BLACKFO
DIVING LIFE
AND TIMES

Andy Blackford

What the critics say about this book

"A sombre testament to the permanent effects of nitrogen narcosis".

– J. Nicholson (1st class Diver)

"We always knew Andrew had a book in him. Whoever let it out has a lot to answer for".

– Mrs Blackford (Snr)

"Even in Sicily, this book would constitute grounds for divorce . . ."

– Solicitor representing Mrs Blackford (Jnr)

"Once I put it down, I couldn't pick it up".

– Norman Mailer

"Very, very funny – very, very moving . . . a coruscating rainbow of tears and laughter".

– Andy Blackford

40 Grays Inn Road
London WC1X 8LR

Cover design and all
illustrations by Rico

Book designed and produced
by Nigel Eaton

Typeset by Graphic Studios (Southern) Ltd,
16b High St, Godalming, Surrey,
and printed by
The Garden City Press Ltd, Letchworth,
Hertfordshire SG6 1JS.

ISBN: 0 946020 09 4

Contents

Dive-speak Directory

ABLJ: Adjustable Buoyancy Life Jacket. A cross between a horse collar and a toilet seat. The ABLJ lets you sink, ascend, or hover in the water, according to how much you inflate or deflate it.

AQUALUNG: A minor miracle that occurs whenever a demand valve is attached to a cylinder of compressed air.

BEAUFORT SCALE: An ascending scale of numbers used to describe the strength of the wind. Where British diving is concerned, the Richter Scale is usually more appropriate.

BENDS: See "Decompression Sickness".

BS-AC: The British Sub-Aqua Club. The "governing body" of the sport in the UK. Developed an internationally respected training system and a safe set of decompression tables.

CONSERVATION: It's hard to imagine, but there was once so much marine life in the Channel that the crabs had to live in tower blocks. The conservationist motto is "live and let live".

DECOBRAIN: Throw away those tiresome tables. This box of tricks lets you dive to impossible depths for hours at a time. Expect to pay over £300 for the novelty of being able to say, "I've left my Brain in the van" – although Fisher Price are bringing out a nice red and yellow one for just £4.99.

DECOMPRESSION SICKNESS: While you dive, little bits of nitrogen get squashed into your body. If you come up too late or too fast, your blood takes on the consistency of boiling coca cola. This kills you.

DEMAND VALVE: No matter how often it's explained, a device that delivers air at the right pressure at any depth has got to be magic. (If it wasn't, you'd either suffocate or explode).

DIVING OFFICER: The font of all wisdom in the branch. A sort of submarine Atilla the Hun. The DO is democratically elected, of course. But then so was Hitler.

DRYSUIT: A quaint piece of usage this. For in my experience drysuits are usually wetter than wetsuits. To exclude water, the drysuit uses seals. Significantly perhaps, seals seldom use drysuits.

GAS LAWS: A proper respect for the Gas Laws is essential. Under Boyle's Law, a first offence carries a maximum fine of £25. With Burke's Law, you can usually get away with community work.

GOODY BAG: The submarine equivalent of the supermarket trolley. ("There's a special offer on lobsters at Mousehole this week"). Closet conservationists sew up the mouths of their goody bags.

INFLATABLE: Air-filled rubber boat, popular among divers. Once on the plane, it's remarkably fast. But sneaking it past the stewardess requires real ingenuity.

MARSHAL: Easily distinguished by the starfish pinned to his chest, the Marshal organises the day's diving. He is blamed for everything, thanked for nothing. The hours are long, the rewards non-existent. The Marshal is a saint or an idiot.

NITROGEN NARCOSIS: See "Rapture of the Deep".

NON-FERROUS: To a certain type of diver, an old porthole is more enticing than the Treasure of the Sierra Madre. He lives in the centre of a diabolical engine room, surrounded by ancient ship's plumbing, tangled machinery, and empty Brasso cans.

OUTBOARD ENGINE: An expensive and incomprehensible device designed to create the illusion of mobility.

PHOTOGRAPHY: Unlike spearfishermen, underwater photographers take hundreds of shots and never hit anything.

POOL: There is more marine life in our Branch training pool than there is in the North Sea.

RAPTURE OF THE DEEP: When you reach a certain depth, something strange happens to your brain. You think you're a horse. Or you recite the prose poems of Patience Strong. Or both. Can be dangerous, or fun, or both.

RUPTURE OF THE STEEP: A common condition afflicting divers who attempt to carry outboard motors up Chesil Beach.

SCALLOP: These delicious shellfish cost 50p a piece at an up-market fishmonger – and about £20 each if you try to catch them yourself. There are scallop banks off Lulworth, but you can't open an account without a reference.

SPEARFISHERS: Whatever happened to *real* men? John Wayne? James Bond? Martina Navratalova? Answer: they took up spearfishing and proved their masculinity at the expense of defenceless marine life. *Spearfishers do it to death!*

SPONGE: A highly successful colonial creature which can be anything from an orange slime to a shapeless, rubbery lump. Sponges are primitive, as life-forms go. Very few pass their accountancy exams.

STAB JACKET: The latest fad in buoyancy aids. Designed to destroy the whole point of diving by making it comfortable and convenient. This year, single-breasted is in. Pierre Cardin favours flared cuffs for that nautical look.

SUB-CUTANEOUS EMPHYSEMA: A truly horrible condition, the exact details of which temporarily elude me.

TRANSIT: An imaginary line drawn between a boat at sea and two landmarks on shore, also usually imaginary. When the boat is positioned at the intersection of two such imaginary lines, it is precisely above an imaginary wreck.

TREASURER: Once a year, the branch treasurer performs a feat more astonishing than the raising of the *Titanic:* he extracts the annual subscription from a bunch of divers.

VAN: Club vans are usually held together by the sticky tape from parking tickets. One branch uses a corporation dust cart powered by a 5hp British Seagull outboard and two hampsters in a treadmill. (see also "Transit").

VHF: Very High Frequency refers to the extraordinary failure rate among boat radios. Indeed, in certain primitive branches, the radio has a significance more religious than practical. (see "Wireless Cults of the Medway Towns").

VISIBILITY: A purely hypothetical concept when applied to British waters, where the translucency of the sea seldom exceeds that of a brick wall.

WEIGHTBELT: 1986, and they're still making weightbelts out of lead. Surely the race that landed a man on the moon can come up with something lighter?

WINDSURFERS: Narcissistic, muscle-bound poseurs much taken to oiling their way into the affections of divers' womenfolk while their partners are busy being *real* men under water.

CHAPTER 1: *Watery awakenings in Runswick Bay*

Early life and times

I'm a slow starter. That's what comes of beginning life in Middlesbrough. I was born in the next bed to William David Callender Dawson, my best friend. He is not a diver, but he is a marvellous painter.

He and I waxed nautical from Day One. Our folks owned holiday homes at Runswick Bay, near Whitby. (Bram Stoker has Dracula flit over its southern headland, a place of truly Gothic desolation.)

We both possessed boats and we were rarely out of them. Mine was a plywood pram called *Lusitania.*

I used to think that Runswick Bay was terribly deep; but, in the single most exciting adventure of my diving career, I explored its plunging abysses with a mask and a snorkel and a stiff new wetsuit. It was a submarine Return of the Native. I was 30 years old, an E&F diver, and I must report that the Mariana Trench of my childhood is nowhere deeper than 10m.

How did I come to take up diving? Quite by accident. Misspent years as economist, rock guitarist, skateboarder, music publisher, journalist, and, latterly, advertising copywriter, filled me with a desire for peace and rural seclusion.

We bought a place in Dorset – a cottage with all the proper subsidences and infestations. I felt a novel coming on.

It was in a dentist's waiting room in Blandford Forum that I read about the course in Goat Handling. I could barely contain my excitment as I pulled up outside the Globe Hotel, Wells-next-the-Sea, and went in search of the man who could show me how to make a going concern of my two goats, Reg and Kendall.

This person turned out to be Derek Ellerby, East Midlands Coach of the BS-AC. And, after a day of incomprehensible lectures, it eventually dawned on me that *Goat* was a misprint for *Boat*. I was now a fully-qualifed coxswain.

After this, diving seemed to follow quite naturally. I will be 36 years old next birthday. I no longer possess a boat. The novel remains unwritten. As the father of Tommy (5) and Nick (2), I am forced to seek my seclusion underwater. I suspect the same is true for many of us; it is not so much a lust for adventure that drives us to dive, as the longing for a little blessed peace and quiet.

Before long, I began to teach others to dive. It was frightening to discover how my own lifesaving skills had deteriorated. Given an emergency of sufficient scale, I could easily have drowned the entire branch.

Andy Blackford
2nd Class Diver, London (No.I) Branch BS-AC
August 1986.

CHAPTER 2: *I get into the sweet shop . . .*

Rapture of the deep

I enjoyed my first tantalising glimpse of the submarine world during a lazy holiday in the Aegean. And no longer than minutes after borrowing a mask and snorkel from a stranger on the shore, I was charging about the beach in a state of shock, jabbering about huge fish and manta rays and how you'd never believe what was going on down there and why hadn't anybody told me?

After a week, I began to tire of peering in on this new world from the outside. I was like a small boy with his nose pressed against a sweet-shop window. I desperately wanted to be down there, a part of it all. Somewhere in the darkest recesses of my nature, the tails were beginning to twitch on Piscean fish genes.

So the following Spring found me enrolling at Willy Halpert's Aquasport dive centre in Eilat, an Israeli resort at the head of the Gulf of Aqaba. I was about to embark on a six-day course in diving with what the purists call Self Contained Underwater Breathing Apparatus (SCUBA).

Now six days is a very short time in which to learn the basic skills of survival in a hostile environment. But at the hands of Willy's instructors, it seemed like an eternity.

Bruce S. Bell was my man. He claimed to be Californian, but I firmly believe he was carved out of an ingot of tungsten steel in Pittsburg. He had come to Eilat for a rest. For six weeks, he had been pulling corpses out of Lake Tahoe – the victims of an avalanche which had decimated a skiing party the previous winter. For each body recovered, he was paid $18.

Ramy, another instructor, was an Israeli. A commando during the last two Middle East wars, he claims to have sunk the entire Egyptian fleet single-handed. Now he found amusement only in trying to drown diving novices.

Arie, another Israeli, derived a morose satisfaction from feeding bits of raw steak to an eight-foot moray eel which lived under a rock off Eilat's Coral Beach.

Aquasport was no kindergarten.

The course was divided equally between theory and practice. Students hit the water at nine, then legged it up the beach to the classroom for lectures. Half-an-hour for lunch, back into the water, back up to the classroom, then home for a beer at sunset.

After two days on this programme, a beer had roughly the same effect as a hydrogen bomb. I was rarely conscious after 9pm.

To begin the course, I had to complete a rigorous swimming test. Actually, it was designed more to check "water confidence" than style. I had to tread water, lie on water, immerse myself in water, tie knots in water, and struggle about in water handicapped by a clump of lead weights.

Once that was out of the way, Snorkel Training began in earnest. Duck dives, forward and backward rolls – and the dreaded clearing of masks. I say "dreaded", but in truth I was the only one on the course to find this simple and vital technique anything less than a walkover.

Sitting on the seabed with the snorkel sticking up into the air, the student removes his face mask, replaces it and clears it of water by exhaling through his nose. Except me. I removed my mask and began to drown.

This was a real problem. My brain reasoned calmly that as long as the snorkel remained firmly in my mouth, then air would reach my lungs. My nose replied: "Sod his mouth, I'm full of water." My brain agreed. "Hell's teeth, we're drowning!" And so I was.

I almost abandoned the course because I simply couldn't seem to master this problem. I beat it by practising endlessly in the hotel swimming pool – sitting in the shallow end while a succession of over-filled bikinis paddled sedately by.

They probably thought I was a pervert, but I didn't care. After two days, I found I could clear my mask. I went back to the sea.

Bruce S. Bell confirmed that I had mastered the technique by pulling off my mask in the deep end of the Gulf of Aqaba. It was a crude, but effective, way of convincing me that as long as

the air supply is stuffed tightly in your gob, you are in absolutely no danger of a watery grave.

By Day Four, we were happily removing masks, regulators – even entire aqualungs – with complete confidence.

This, despite the horror stories which formed a substantial chunk of our lecture programme. Just when you thought it was safe to go back in the water, you were bombarded with gruesome descriptions of Burst Lung, Subcutaneous Emphysema, Caisson's Disease, Pneumothorax, Carbon Monoxide Poisoning and a host of other, horrible, conditions which would set in immediately if you didn't listen to Bruce.

Confronted with Boyle's Law, Henry's Law, Archimedes' Principle, and a set of dive tables, I made an interesting discovery. I shared a brain with an African Violet. Ten years had elapsed since I'd taxed my intellect with anything more demanding than *Jackanory*. My main worry now was how I was going to avoid Nitrogen Narcosis – a treacherous form of over-confidence – while still remembering to breathe.

Talking of narcosis, Bruce S. Bell was once confronted with a severe case at 40 metres. His buddy had felt an enormous wave of pity for a passing eel because it didn't have an aqualung. So he removed his own and gave it to the fish. A bold show of support for the Animal Rights Movement – and a near-fatal one – but that's the 'narks'.

In the event, Bruce S. Bell performed an emergency ascent with his drowning buddy, who experienced no ill effects whatsoever. The said Bell, on the other hand, spent four days in a recompression chamber with an acute "bend", the cost of his rescue. Life's like that.

The climax of the course was the Test Dive at Moses Rock – an astonishing coral outcrop off the beach near Eilat.

As we reached the Rock, we were immersed in shoals of zebra fish, goat and parrot fish, groupers, wrasse and triggers. It was as if they'd glanced at their watches and agreed: "OK, it's time for Willy's Test Dive. Lunch is served!"

Our instructors had stuffed the pockets of their lifejackets with pitta bread and soon the fish were literally eating out of our hands.

The corals formed a fantastic garden of pinks and violets and greens. Ferns of web-like delicacy fanned upwards towards the rippling sunlight. Great heads of brain coral, thousands of years old yet for all the world like abstract modern sculpture, made a fantastic landscape of cliffs and caves, ridges and ravines.

The paranoia of the past six days melted away as we became totally absorbed in the flora and fauna of this magical garden. In a tiny cave, a lion fish swayed in sun-like splendour. One of our party alarmed a puffer fish, who blew himself up into a spiky sphere and patiently endured a gentle game of volley-ball at our hands. A couple of clown fish, sole residents of a particularly poisonous type of anemone, sallied out gamely to joust with my wrist compass.

We were captivated. Our delighted grins broke the seals of our masks and I had to do a spot of mask-clearing in earnest.

Not so funny was the written examination. "Calculate the partial pressure of oxygen at 50 metres". "Your partner is exhibiting a bloody froth at the mouth: Would you (a) perform an emergency ascent? (b) remove his watch on the grounds that he won't be needing it any more?". That sort of thing.

Miraculously, we all passed. The nightmare evaporated in a week-long orgy of sub-aqua exploration in which I buddied up with a lady parachutist who had once worked in Australia as a bulldozer driver; in which the glory of the Red Sea opened up like a rose; in which, like April cygnets, we found our way in the water, learned a little grace and poise.

Not least, we grew to savour that exquisite moment when, after a rich and satisfying dive, you struggle out of a soggy wetsuit into the golden warmth of the desert and rip the ring-pull on a can of iced Macabee lager.

Two years later, the Sinai reverted to Egypt under the terms of the Camp David agreement. The worst fears of the diving fraternity have proved to be unfounded. You can still experience the glories of the Red Sea coral during competitively-priced safaris and cruises.

I've never been back. I quickly discovered that British waters possess their own brooding enchantment – that the Western Isles of Scotland, for instance, are richer in marine life than most tropical waters, and certainly less frequently visited by divers.

Over the years, the quaking apprehension of those first dives in Israel has mellowed to a healthy instinct for self-preservation.

My wetsuit is held together with string and bubble gum. I always get the most comfortable seat in the inflatable. I no longer feel that obsessive enthusiasm that makes you dive in septic tanks in Janaury just to get wet.

Some years, I get to dive a lot. Some years, not so often as I'd like. But even if I never got to dive again, I would count myself immeasurably richer for the experience.

CHAPTER 3: *The perils of kit fixation*

Days of brine and hoses

Do me a favour. Next time you bump into me within a mile's radius of a dive-shop, get me the hell out of it – and fast. Use any means at your disposal. Appeal to my reason. Play upon my emotions. Strike me just behind the ear with a lump hammer. Grasp me firmly in the pistol grip and tow me to a taxi. Tell the cabbie to dump me penniless at the head of Wensleydale with no possible access to dive-shops, chandleries or mail-order catalogues.

For those ranks of gleaming, virgin cylinders, those spotless squads of parading wetsuits, those banks of watches, torches, clasps and compasses – they work upon my wallet like boiling water on a scallop.

Dive-shop proprietors see me coming. Something in my glazed, unseeing stare reminds them of a mackerel on a gaff hook.

They start work with tempting morsels – gaudy little *hors d'oevres* concealing barbs that will rip out your Diners' Club card from 20m. Webbing compass-straps. Pens for writing down jokes underwater. Pendants in fool's gold, containing details of your blood group, IQ and religion.

Mesmerised by such trinkets, I quickly enter a state of deep hypnosis. The skilled assistant will now step up the assault with special aqualung hats, phosphorescent Taiwanese dive-boots, shark-repellent after-shaves.

If it's been invented, I'll buy it. If it hasn't, I'll put down a deposit.

It's a depressingly common syndrome, this jackdaw obsession with acquiring bits of kit.

Actually, it's even more common among a certain sort of

land-based amateur photographer – the kind who looks like a photo montage of Jodrell Bank and incessantly subjects you to slide-shows that would dwarf the uncut version of *Alexander The Great.*

"Ah! Kilimanjaro at dawn! f.16 at 1/250 sec on 400 asa Fuji, up-rated to 800 and triple-solarised with a 150-fixated catalyst," (drone, drone).

But the worst of both worlds is undoubtedly the kit-obsessed *underwater* photographer. Getting him out of the boat and into the water is like launching Skylab. He resembles a nightmare victim of spare-part surgery; a Christmas tree of carabinos, bristling with the cold foilage of our micro-processed age.

He is, incidentally, prime contender for Most Boring Dive Buddy Of All Time. As bar after precious bar dribbles away, he will lay, prone as a brain-damaged bloater, awaiting tiny alterations in the state of some hydroid, while you dream of wrenching off his air and practising assisted descents with his carcass till the spider crabs get his extremities.

Fortunately, I am saved from his special addiction, by raw poverty. I'd have to sell rotgut to the Apaches before I could afford a Nikonos with all its glittering optical entourage. And I'm damned if I'll settle for second best.

For surely there is an exquisite pathos in the spectacle of some poor lummock with an Instamatic in a poly bag, trying to shoot the sequel to *Blue Water, White Death* between B and C lessons in the shallow end of Balham Baths.

No. For me, it's Al bloody Giddings or nowt.

Of course, it's a fact approaching natural law that every excess has its opposite. Obesity demands its anorexia, mania its depression, and so on. And so it is with Kit Fixation.

For every diver who needs a caddy to lug his dive-bag about, there's a rugged ascetic who believes that the invention of the demand valve took most of the fun out of diving.

I met ours on my first club dive. He bought me a pint of lager and himself a half of ginger beer. Then he treated me to an hour's worth of riveting reminiscences about diving as it used to be done, way back when men were Men and women merely a disturbing rumour.

It was a highly personalised account, to be sure, liberally doused with nostalgia for times long gone.

A sort of one-man "Days of Brine and Hoses", if you like.

"Aqualung?" he'd snort. "Aqualung? My dear fellow. I've

been diving since I was three. The father taught me. No aqualungs about in those days, I can tell you. Just an old vacuum cleaner. All we could afford, you understand? Still, we made do." And so on.

He claimed he'd made his first DV out of wood. And that, as he surfaced from a two-hour dive in the Solway Firth, he was shot in the head by a fisherman who took him for a seal.

Happily, like Life itself, the whole caboodle magically balances out in the end. The great majority of divers are sane, code-abiding, middle-of-the-roaders who buy precisely that amount of kit which will keep them safe, warm and versatile underwater.

And around the periphery, there will always hover the weave-your-own-fins merchant; and the bloke with the combined snorkel and flare gun.

But that's entertainment. Part of the rich pageant we call diving. For all the world's a first stage and . . . *pshaw!* Who gives a fig for philosophy? For West Wales beckons. *Hither! Hither!* The nipper's settling down nicely in the boarding kennel. I've taken out a second mortgage on a full tank of four-star. The Black Pig (my ancient neo-Gothic cylinder) awaits me, stamped and rumbled, at the dive-shop. And I must away.

Besides, I hear they're offering an 8 per cent discount on those argon-loaded, 300m-tested Teflon elbow protectors from El Salvador that even now are changing the face of the sport for ever.

CHAPTER 4: *My wreck dive with Whitby BS-AC*

Rock bottom in Saltwick Bay

Seldom does an issue of *Diver* go by without some lavishly-illustrated item of tropical exotica. It takes only 500 words on "How I Wrestled with English-Speaking Porpoises in the Galapagos" or "The Day I Found the Holy Grail on the Wreck of the *Marie Celeste* in Fifty Metres of Gin-Clear Water off Paradise Atol" to throw me into a fit of burning jealousy.

Bitterly I recall my excitement as I stumbled on the sunken pedallo in the boating pond at Peasholme Park, Scarborough. Or the potent cocktail of terror and awe that overwhelmed me when I came face to face with that newt in the Blue Lagoon, Bletchley.

Then I pull myself up short. Hold fast there, I inwardly exclaim! Just because you don't spend 6 months a year and a king's ransom swanning around the coral seas on a yacht with a platoon of bronzed Danish models and more photographic gear than Steven Spielberg, that doesn't give you a licence to whine.

No, sir! Rather spare a thought for Whitby BS-AC. Recall the time you joined them for a wreck dive, I tell myself. And suddenly the boating lake at Peasholme Park is invested with an aura of mystery and adventure; Bletchley shimmers on the mind's horizon like Eldorado, beckoning, beckoning . . .

Whitby BS-AC was founded by a caucus of criminally-insane escapees.

You have to be insane to dive regularly in the North Sea. Twenty-two stone mega-men are dragged through special courses in the highlands of Scotland to prepare them for North Sea diving. They're fed on a diet of dew and sharp stones. They have to beat themselves up twice a day and carry Ben Nevis to

Aberdeen and back just to earn the quart of tepid paint stripper that serves as a buck-me-up at the end of a day's training.

To complete this crash course in rubber-clad masochism the successful graduate must dismember an entire *SAS* regiment in front of a panel of judges before he is allowed to experience nil vis, hypothermia, and acute schitzoid paranoia, 100m beneath the sputum-encrusted piles of the oil rig *Esso Unmentionable.*

And that's only the half of it. Anyway, Whitby BS-AC divers do it for fun!

On the day I scrounged a dive with Whitby, our dive-site was in Saltwick Bay, a mile to the south of the town itself.

Saltwick Bay doesn't deserve the name. As a piece of coast, it's about as appealing as Dunkirk during the Evacuation.

We kitted up at the top of a 200ft cliff. Then we staggered down an alpine path to the 'beach'.

My buddy was called Martin. He looked like a John Wayne clone, with hands like hams. He'd obviously stripped his wetsuit straight off the carcass of a killer whale.

Martin was a man of few words. In fact, for the first hour of our partnership, he was a man of no words at all. His vocabulary was restricted to a sort of universal monosyllable – like this: 'Nunk'.

I was quickly cast in the role of Visiting London Playboy Joker. When three pounds of my body weight evaporated en route to the beach, I said aimiably, "Christ, thank heaven that's over. Can I go home now?". I grinned, (I thought) disarmingly. Martin said: "Nnnnnk". Martin's wife said, "Aye! Y'ave t'be FIT t'dive wit' OUR cloob!" A sudden chill pierced me to the quick. Whitby BS-AC was Serious.

After some muttered conspiracy, the TO pointed to the horizon (where the sea was). "We'll go in over there," he said.

I dragged myself across half a mile of shale flats slick with sea grass. My wetsuit felt like a zip-on pressure cooker. My aqualung was one of those boulders that giants shunt up and down mountains in Greek mythology. In a nutshell, it was purgatory.

As we neared the dive site, we noticed a converted trawler, apparently moored over our wreck. It flew the blue-and-white flag. An inflatable bobbed in the foreground.

Martin and the TO strode manfully off across the winkle beds to check out the situation.

They returned. The TO spoke. "We're not bloody divin' off

'ere. The wreck's swarmin' wit KRAUTS!"

The alternative wreck was a good quarter mile away across the shale, winkles and soggy sea grass. Recall the scene in *Bridge Over The River Kwai* where the Nips drag Alec out of the oven every now and then, torture him with false promises of freedom, then cruelly stuff him back into prison?

When we finally reached the chosen site, we had to fight our way through kelp stalks like small trees. I would trip on a kelp stalk and flounder about in the shallows. I'd regain my footing for an instant before being flattened by a Bondai-standard roller and whipped back into the nearest kelp-bed.

After an eternity, we were clear of waves and weed. With his typical flair for words, Martin punched out a single thumbs-down signal. "Right-ho!", I warbled.

In the minutes that followed, I developed profound sympathy for the pinball. We cannoned from rock to rock, helpless and winded, until a freak wave dragged us out and down – down into a bewildering maelstrom, the colour and consistency of taramasalata.

We hung like grim death to our buoy-line as we were spun, out of control, into the dizzying depths of the North Sea. This was like nothing I'd ever dived before. There were no reference points – no ups, no downs. Just this endless, spiralling plummet into the abyss. I half expected to see strange, blind crabs and giant, irridescent squid from an Age before Ages.

Instead, I saw nothing. Not even Our Leader – and certainly not a wreck. Eventually, I hit bottom. Hardly daring to look, I inspected my depth gauge – a little under five metres.

Then my mask came abruptly up against Martin's. We peered into one another's eyes like guppies in adjacent fishbowls before Martin gave the thumbs-up signal. I responded vigorously in the affirmative.

At the surface, we took a little time to scrape the slime of centuries from our faces. Then Martin spat out his demand valve and lifted his mask. When he grinned, it was like the sun coming through. He spoke. Just one word – but it was all the more meaningful for being the only one he'd spoken all day.

"Fascinatin'," he said.

In that single withering word there was condensed all the stoical ruggedness of the Norsemen. A sort of grim satisfaction that Life really was as rotten as you'd secretly suspected it to be.

And I knew, in a sudden blaze of intuition, that in Whitby,

Hartlepool, Seahouses, or Bridlington, there would always be one sad, craggy man inching his way into an icy wetsuit beside a storm-torn desolation of sea.

And this knowledge never fails to cheer me up when I scan the *Holidays Abroad* column at the back of *Diver*, and count the noughts on the prices.

For compared to Saltwick Bay, Stoney Cove is certainly the Red Sea, and the Inner Mulberry at Pagham is the Great Barrier Reef.

CHAPTER 5: *Bank Holiday theft at Bovisand*

Crime and punishment

There were so many divers in the water, the sea level rose two inches in Plymouth Sound.

The atmosphere was one of happy, all-pervading chaos. Red-faced men in Morris Marinas tried in vain to outstare hard-nosed commandos in one-ton trucks.

The jetty was the stage for a curiously graceful ballet of divers' wives performing nine-point pirouettes in their Renault 5s around great tangles of abandoned boat-trailers.

The weather was bright and sunny, pierced by a bitter North wind. To stand unprotected on the harbour wall was like being stabbed in the back by a smiling man.

DOs from Slough and Hampstead and Dunstable and Sale bustled little knots of ducklings into the water for their first dip outside the nursery of the pool.

The coffee from the cafeteria had clearly been developed at Porton Down for use against Argentinians.

On the face of it, it was a perfectly ordinary Bank Holiday at Bovisand . . . There were, however, two important differences between this year and any other.

Firstly, about one half of the divers present wore drysuits – the result of the extraordinary and sudden success of the Typhoon "membrane" and its imitators.

As it happens, my own drysuit was about as effective as a pair of fishnet tights. The water gushed contemptuously past the seals, through my woolly bear and thence across every cringing millimetre of flesh. When I finally slopped back along the harbour, I looked like one of those plastic bags they put goldfish in at fairgrounds. Ah, me.

And now, on a more sombre note, the second major

difference between Bovi '82 and Bovis Previous. In four days enough gear was swiped to kit up two battalions of the SBS.

Put it down for two seconds and it miraculously disappeared, spirited away to some great Jackdaw's Nest In The Sky.

If you own a Cortina, take heed. Not only will any Cortina key fit your boot, but so, apparently, will the keys to any Rover, Pontiac, De Dion, Cord or Moskvitch. Ignorance of this fact cost one of our E&F boys his ABLJ.

I lost my credit cards. And Excalibur, my mighty knife.

I pity the thief. I had taken the precaution of smearing its lethally-honed plutonium blade with Actovil 63, a viral culture of withering toxicity which can reduce a normal, healthy criminal to a kilo of quivering aspic in less time than it takes to say "ello, 'ello, 'ello!"

Also, I would urge the unfortunate creature who made off with my snorkel to seek medical advice at the first possible opportunity. He very probably has Legionnaire's Disease.

I say this only because I seem to have Legionnaire's Disease. One theory is that I contracted the bacterium from water vapour inhaled through one of the branch's Bakelite oxygen rebreather sets, purchased at the turn of the century from the Imperial War Museum and now hired to any member subscribing to a medical insurance scheme.

Terminal diseases apart, this sudden burgeoning of felony is a sad reflection upon our times.

Excalibur went from the dormitory floor. The thief had penetrated the inner sanctum of the Branch-in-Exile, and made off with my most prized possession (after a blue drape jacket once worn by Johnny Kidd).

Yet even in times of adversity the human spirit has a knack of coming up trumps. Tony, a pillar of the club and a man of great generosity, announced his personal explanation of this spate of petty crime: "I don't think it's divers who are to blame. I think it's people *dressed up* as divers!" It makes you ashamed to be a careworn old cynic.

Another, less generous explanation was offered by our Training Officer: "It's bloody *windsurfers*, innit?"

Anyway, whoever you are, you made the Easter weekend a little less euphoric than it should have been. May your stoats all be sterile and your innards rot upon the Street Of a Thousand Nasal Obstructions.

None of which will bring back Excalibur, of course. Or my Excess Card, or my season ticket to the adventure playground, or the little tag that said, "I am a diver. Please lie down and adopt the coma position." Gone, all of these, forever.

I don't know about you, but I'm going to tear the diving stickers from my car windows. And I'm going to have an alarm fitted which will raise the dead should anyone tamper with doors, bonnet or boot. And I'm going to staple every piece of equipment I still possess to one of those loose folds of flesh which mar my otherwise perfect body.

And if any petty thief dares to dress up as a diver and knock off any more of my gear, I'm going to run amok in an orgy of revenge that will make *Death Wish 2* look like *Bambi.*

Evenin', all.

CHAPTER 6: *I nearly become a statistic*

Close to the edge

Saturday, 8am – blue skies, oily sea. The *Thomas* is one of three boats bound for the wreck of the *James Egan Layne.*

Our club outboard had coughed and spluttered at high revs on Friday. But exhaustive blasts in the Bovi test tank revealed no serious malfunction, and the engine was duly passed.

Two hundred metres offshore and the engine began to gag on an open throttle. Sensibly, David Sisman ran her back to base for a check-out.

The fault was untraceable. We agreed to run out to a local dive-site rather than risk an hour's meander, off the plane, to the *James Egan Layne.*

A little disappointed, I steeled myself for another 60 minutes' exposure to a freshening North-easter.

A mile offshore, the sea was bright with white caps. Spray splattered against my soaking wetsuit, and despite the bright spring sunshine, I soon became a little chilled and a little apprehensive. I would gratefully have pressed an imaginary "abort" button and transported myself to the Bovisand cafeteria.

It was as bad as that.

"I'll be OK once I'm in," I argued mutely with myself. And so, doing that, I deliberately suppressed a natural danger signal.

I was both anxious and shivering when I flopped into a Beaufort Scale 3 sea.

Hitting the water was like rolling out of bed into a bath of crushed ice. Instantly, my lungs refused to operate.

Slattery (RN) was loving every minute of it. But I had to

delay the descent. I was gasping for air, but inhaling only a gaseous mixture of cold and anxiety.

Where do you draw the line? Few divers go down without a little thrill of apprehension. Indeed, how many of us would dive at all, were it not for that irresistible tingle of danger that sets our sport apart from volleyball and international dominoes?

I shrugged off my worries, dumped the air in my ABLJ, and commenced my descent.

Almost immediately, my mask flooded. Simple. Flooded mask. Recall training. Head back, mask-top depressed, nasal exhalation. Mask cleared.

I can *hear* the rattle of bubbles as the sea runs under the seal on my port cheek and refloods the mask. Laboriously, I clear my ears, check my position, void my mask and recommence my descent.

Visibility at 20m was relatively good. But the sun had ducked behind clouds and the greyish gloom of the bottom did not inspire one to burst into a chorus of *The Sound of Music.*

Icy fingers of freezing Channel crept up my arms and down my back. As thermal protection, my gloves were about as effective as a goody-bag. One of my boots was split. I wasn't really dressed for the job.

Around the perimeter of my mask, I felt the cold as a sharp, sinal pain.

I was tense with cold and anxiety. Breathing was becoming a real effort. My attempts to adjust buoyancy resulted in my swallowing a good half-pint of brine.

And then came the subtle psychological water-shed – the line between a stable situation and a potentially unstable one.

A small voice demanded, "What if this turned into an 'incident' – one of those matter-of-fact horror stories from the DOs' Conference report?"

Questions like this are apt to be self-fulfilling prophecies. Instead of calmly analysing what was, after all, a perfectly ordinary set of circumstances, my mind was already grappling with imaginary catastrophes.

I had to go up. I ceased trying to clear my mask. It was pointless, anyway. I signalled ascent to Nick, who shrugged and began to reel in the buoyline.

By now, I was effectively blinded by water. After what seemed an eternity of upward progress my fins scraped the bottom. I hadn't moved an inch.

Panic was not a million miles away, but good sense prevailed. I allowed a little air into my ABLJ and set out once again for the surface. Cold and tension had resulted in a painful cramp in one leg. I felt utterly miserable.

Just as a mask full of water had disguised the fact that I wasn't ascending, now it disguised the fact that I was going up too fast. But I noticed that my surroundings were becoming rapidly lighter. A glance downwards afforded a glimpse of yellow – Nick's ABLJ, some 3m below me.

In an instant, I'd dumped all of my air and at last began to ascend at an ordinary rate.

When I reached the surface, I was exhausted, chilled to the marrow, more than a little frightened, but otherwise unharmed. Our bottom-time had been a mere five minutes. It had seemed like a lifetime.

The entire grisly carry-on, though, was an education and a source of invaluable experience. Among other things, it taught me:

1. That good boots and gloves contribute enormously to general, all-over warmth.
2. That cold is not merely a physical discomfort, it is a powerful depressant which lowers the physical threshold of panic, inhibits the ability to think clearly and liberates all sorts of suppressed anxiety.
3. That while the sensation of impending panic is an unpleasant one, it has the effect of alerting one to the danger of uncontrolled behaviour; presumably, a hefty dose of adrenalin restores order to the thought processes, and allows one to behave rationally once more.
4. That so-called "incidents" can develop with terrifying rapidity from seemingly minor beginnings; after all, my DV hadn't packed up, I hadn't become entangled in weed and I hadn't lost my buddy.
5. That one should never ignore the little warning signals that say, "You're cold and uncomfortable, and you don't want to go diving." If you're unhappy at the start of a dive, things aren't going to get any better underwater.

All in all the experience was a valuable one. In a way, I'm glad it happened. I believe it reinforced my respect for the water and what it can do to me. And it also provided an encouraging answer to a question that, I'm sure, must nag us all from time to time: *If something went wrong, would I be able to cope?*

I did. I saw panic, but I didn't submit to it. I acted correctly. I tried to clear my mask. It didn't work (the clip at the side was undone, as it turns out). I was cold and miserable so I decided to abort the dive, and signalled to my buddy accordingly. I had trouble ascending, so I partially inflated my ABLJ. I ascended too quickly, so I dumped my air and reached the surface safely.

That afternoon, I dropped into 15m feeling calm, happy and secure, to enjoy my best dive of the weekend.

CHAPTER 7: *The high price of diving*

The world's most expensive crab

I don't suppose there's a diver in the world who hasn't dreamed of stumbling on some priceless underwater treasure.

A brass-bound chest of Spanish doubloons. The dowry of some forgotten Maya princess in emeralds the size of water melons. The ship's telegraph from Noah's Ark.

Imagine, then, my triumph as I joined the ranks of that elite for whom the dream has become reality.

For this year, off the Cornish coast in seven metres of kelp-laced curd, I happened on the find of my diving career.

No antiquity, this. No trove of gold or ancient artefact. My treasure was infinitely more precious.

In fact, as edible crabs go, it was probably the most valuable in the history of marine exploration.

It happened like this ...

Whitsun weekend. Left London on Friday evening, five minutes behind the rest of the capital's 10 million inhabitants. Paused at filling station in Hammersmith and marvelled at the insatiable thirst of my car .... £23.65.

Near Swindon on the M4, everybody stopped. It was like being on a vast Scalextric track in a power cut. In two hours, we travelled nine miles.

I limped into a service area for a spot of R & R. I was dizzy with fatigue.

As luck would have it, the service area was being used by a film production company. They seemed to be casting extras for a sequel to *Night Of The Living Dead*

What is it about those places? Do they offer bulk discount to morons? Do you get a special price on a cold hamburger if you're prepared to wear calf-length flared trousers?

I had to get out of the place. I bolted down a drab Welsh Rarebit . . . . £4.95.

The fog closed in at Saltash. I careered blindly on for a few hair-raising miles, then surrendered. I hadn't bargained on bed & breakfast, but I have an agreement with my tent. I won't try to erect it in anything fiercer than Force 6.

The B & B was up to par. The night was punctuated by mild, electric shocks from the brushed nylon sheets. I found the spare toilet roll under a pink woolly poodle in the bathroom. Mrs Figgins couldn't "be doin' with cheques" because she didn't "'old with 'em" . . . . £9.50.

Dropped into Petropolis, Lostwithiel, for another fix of gas. I'm not saying my car's heavy on fuel, but the gauge is marked in arms and legs.

Reached Marazion, 9.30 am. Was confronted by a scene of utter desolation. The rain swept horizontally in from the Atlantic. St Michael's Mount, home of the great Marks & Spencer empire, was barely discernible through the fret. Of the rest of London Branch, there was not so much as a hint.

I retired to a prefabricated cafe on the waterfront. Incredibly, in this remote Cornish outpost, Dot and Eth Polcranny have pioneered a whole new approach to haute cuisine. This is neither the time nor the place to describe their methods in detail: suffice to say that it involves fossilising fragments of reconstituted pork in a skip of cold dripping . . . . £3.85.

Bought industrial catering pack of Rennies . . . . £1.90.

Lamorna Cove is whipped by hurricane-force winds to the consistency of Cornish clotted cream. Nobody volunteered to be the strawberry jam.

Retired to the *Goat & Mallet* for a quiet drink with a few close friends. Bought a round . . . . £23.65.

Next morning, the wind had dropped. We found a lee shore at Porthoustock and kitted up.

Porthoustock must once have been a quiet and pretty cove, embraced as it is by two horn-like protruberances on the flank of the Lizard.

Then some bright spark decided there was a fortune to be made in grey rocks, so they piled monstrous concrete block-houses, one on each headland.

Grey rocks didn't catch on after all. And since reinforced concrete is even more costly to pull down than it is to put up, the blockhouses remain – as harsh and drear a tombstone as any stillborn enterprise could hope for.

I stood my aqualung on a bit of grey rock. It fell over, of course, and landed in such a way as to fracture an LP hose at the first stage of my demand valve. A simple little hose, it hardly deserved the 30-mile drive through Bank Holiday traffic on single-track roads to replace it .... £7.30.... and to refill the bottle .... £1.20.

The dive wasn't great. The seals on my drysuit, I discovered, had degenerated into Marmite.

Fortunately, I always carry a wetsuit as a last ditch reserve. In fact, it looked as if I'd kept it in the last ditch since the last time I wore it, five years ago.

In 1980, I spent four nights a week playing in a band. I lugged tons of amplification equipment about and swam 20 lengths a day. I weighed approximately 20 pounds less than I do today. Even then, my wetsuit was a trifle on the snug side.

I mixed up a thick paste of talc and water and smeared it all over my limbs. I press-ganged four strong men. I squirmed and wriggled and cursed and gasped.

I temporarily dislocated my right thumb, trying to hook the cuff of the suit over my heel.

In the end, I got it on. My upper arms projected at 90 degrees from my trunk, my forearms dangling helplessly down from my elbows.

The hood forced my head down into my chest cavity and the jacket bent my shoulders into a perfect hemisphere. I needn't describe the effects on my privates.

I looked like a cross between Max Wall and Richard III.

I'd forgotten to buy a dive ticket, so I had to pay full whack for the trip .... £2.50.

It's hard to get a duff dive off the Manacles. You have to be a real pro. Here's how we did it.

Two distinct groups of rocks stood proud of the 6 ft ground swell and the vicious cross-chop. One was surrounded by inflatables. The water between them seethed with blob buoys.

The other group of rocks was deserted except for one waiting Zodiac. The cox of this solitary boat hailed us:

"I wouldn't bother 'ere, mate. Seven metres of bleedin' kelp, that's all."

Our handler frowned. "Hello hello. What's he trying to hide? Let's call his bluff. Kit up and go."

We kitted up and went. We hit bottom in thick kelp at 7m.

At first, the dive gave no hint of the majesty that was to unfold. It held its cards very close to its chest.

I found a sink-edge protector in turquoise polypropylene, circa 1979. My buddy wrestled to extricate an empty Savlon tube from a cranny.

And then I saw it. The crab. Fortunately, it didn't see me. Years of living in Cornwall's only naff bit of diving terrain had made him careless. There was no extended interplay of bluff and counterbluff – no intricate joust of crab hook against pincer. I just grabbed him by the backlegs and stuffed him in my goody bag.

As we returned to the dive site, the weather began to clear. The dank mat of cloud evaporated in brilliant sunshine.

Soon, the air would be heavy with the reek of Ambre Solaire, the foreshore rosy with the flesh of scorched telephonists from Bromley.

Whereas I would be stuck behind an "L" registration Allegro on the A38 in a mobile tandoori oven. For I had to be back at the grindstone first thing Tuesday morning.

It took me ten-and-a-half hours to drive from Land's End to London. And two tanks of gas .... £47.30.

And a special, joke meal of recycled sycamore bark at a Moron Centre .... £4.95.

The puncture wouldn't have cost me a penny to repair, had the spare been inflated .... £23.24.

So far, the crab had cost me £211.64.

This works out at a little under £14 an ounce. Which puts crab meat in the same league as myrrh, caviar and unrefined plutonium.

All the more poignant, then, when the bag with the crab in it slipped into the recess for the spare wheel. So that, when I dropped the duff tyre in, it reduced the crab to a brown, malodorous paste, riddled with shards of broken shell.

That's the joy of diving though, isn't it – the warm feeling of familiarity when everything falls expensively apart?

For diving is a perfect microcosm of life. And every expedition confirms one's worst suspicions: namely, that the world is a rat trap, all endeavour pointless, and any promise of pleasure a cruel illusion.

CHAPTER 8: *A year of super-aqua exploits*

Anything to report?

‘It is with immense pleasure that I present this, the first Annual Report of the newly-created *BS-AC* – the British Super-Aqua Club.

The *BS-AC*, of course, was founded as a response to feelings expresed by certain members of the British Sub-Aqua Club who felt an understandable aversion to water.

Sub-aqua clubs, they maintained, are all very well. But at the end of the day one can't avoid getting absolutely soaked. Recent research reveals that getting absolutely soaked is bound to end in tears. Getting even a *bit* soaked has been directly linked with the incidence of Botulism, Green Monkey Fever, and Legionnaires' Disease.

Under the inspired leadership of London No. 1 Branch, these spontaneous stirrings of discontent were forged into a united front: The Campaign for the Advancement of Dry Sports (CADS).

Who would have guessed that a new sporting movement of global significance would emerge from that first, historic canasta drive, held 150 miles from the sea in the back room of a Sheffield surgical appliance shop?

It was in June the following year that London Branch took the plunge (or rather didn't), cancelled a particularly wet dive in Dorset, and boldly embarked upon the first ever dry dive.

Morden is a charming little South London suburb, notable for its historic tube station and its fine, rococo laundromat. Among the famous personages who have avoided Morden are Gerald Harper, Winifred Atwell and James Hanratty. The town's enviable situation at the southern end of the Northern

Line makes it an ideal dry diving site.

And so it was that at 9.30 am on June 16 that our little band of pioneering sportsmen handed in their tickets at the High Street Exit and established base camp beneath the dreaded West Face of Mothercare.

After much discussion, our DO had agreed to permit the use of very-dry-indeed-suits on the condition that the wearer and his buddy were familiar with lapels and emergency fly buttons.

Most of us wore Burton or Austin Reed models, but I was experimenting with a lightweight design, purchased in the 1979 C&A spring event.

After the usual routine of buddy checks (shoe laces, ties, small change, etc), we wandered through a fabulous wonderworld of teeming wildlife, equalled only in its dazzling variety by Peterborough and, perhaps, the Medway Towns.

Within moments we were surrounded by shoals of housewife, wages clerk and accountant – specimens of every conceivable size, shape and colour. We were constantly amazed by their fearless approaches. It is sad to think that it will take only a few brutal onslaughts by gangs of greedy spearfishers to destroy this childlike trust forever.

Our deep appreciation of all we encountered was heightened, as ever, by a keen awareness of the perils attendant on our voyage into a forbidden and hostile environment. Nick Slattery was almost crushed by a rogue Morris Marina. Jerry Clarke was chased by a wasp; and, of course, the threat of carbon monoxide poisoning was never far from our minds.

We employed the services of a native dive guide, Mrs Smedhurst, who turned out to be an invaluable asset. She led us to within 10m of the Huddersfield and Bradford Building Society and, with the unerring instinct of the born dry diver, managed to drop us straight on to the *Dog and Fox*, just behind the Essoldo in Grime Street.

Finefare lived up to its awesome reputation. I quickly filled my goody bag with cream crackers and returned with a trolley to sample the treasures of the fabled Cooked Meats Department.

Our second dive was to be a shallow one. While we had observed the 'no-depression' limits, two of our party were experiencing mild symptoms of depression, having spent 10 minutes in the basement of the Tennessee Pancake House.

I had used up all but 50p during the first dive, and most of us were running seriously short. So I volunteered to get our wallets filled. At first, the outlook seemed bleak. But eventually I found a small tobacconist's kiosk and, with the aid of a speargun, I managed to persuade the proprietor to fill our wallets to a modest fifty pounds per square inch.

The objective of our second dive was to search for intelligent life on the Morden/Colliers Wood border. However, moments after kitting up, the heavens opened and a torrential downpour threatened to ruin our very-dry-indeed-suits.

As dive leader, I was prepared to take no chances. I inflated my umbrella and signalled the others to do likewise.

Within minutes, we were safely installed in the no-smoking compartment of a northbound train – tired, satisfied, and very dry indeed.

We had intended to de-brief over a jar at the *Perseverance*, but the landlord refused to serve us with empty glasses. It was immediately clear that he had thrown in his lot with the 'wet' boys, and the search for a dry pub is now a matter of the utmost urgency.

It only remains for me to add that the next AGM of the British Super-Aqua Club will be held in Death Valley, Arizona, at noon, August 6.'

Andy Blackford,
Honorary Secretary, British Super-Aqua Club.

CHAPTER 9: *Marine identification for dry divers*

Dry characters

Nineteen eighty five has been a great year for dry diving. There has been little or no incentive, after all, to visit the coast. At the height of the summer, I recorded nine metres of water on the M3, and was forced to decompress for ten minutes at the Fleet service area.

And so, with the support of the climate, the sport has advanced in leaps and bounds.

It's hard to believe that only a year has passed since the BS-AC expedition to Leeds, when, clad in primitive, lightweight lounge suits from the Burton Spring Event, we dived the famous North Wall of Tesco, opposite the *Torch and Three Rodents* in Garibaldi Street.

Dry diving was transformed, of course, by the introduction of Gucci loafers in 7mm alligator hide. And there can be no doubt that much unnecessary suffering has been avoided by the development of the super-aqua safety shirt – a remarkable piece of protective clothing for use around conventional "wet diving" sites.

On the front of the shirt, in nine-inch lettering, is embroidered the legend: *I'd like to help*. Whereas, on the reverse side, it reads: *But I'm afraid I've got a touch of the old trouble.*

Work on the club project has proceeded apace this season, with a 90 per cent turn-out on most dives. However, the task of draining the vast beer reservoirs beneath the *Cat and Hacksaw* in Shroton Street has proved more taxing than was originally suspected. Despite continuous pumping and drinking by club members, success seems as far away as ever. Nevertheless, the committee wishes to express its profound gratitude to those "old faithfuls" who have turned up twice a week, rain or shine, to lend a hand in "the great work".

This year, too, we have been able to add to our stock of club equipment. All our members should benefit from our three dozen new bottles, for instance. They include a case of the Côtes de Roussillon '78 that went down so nicely with the venison at last year's AGM.

Our Equipment Officer also managed to purchase four new inflatables from a little place off Soho Square. He informs me that two of them have real hair.

But it is the huge advances in supermarine biology which really make 1985 a red letter year in the annals of the British Super-Aqua Club.

Extensive research among the hordes of "wet divers" populating our shores has revealed an eco-system very similar to the one beneath the waves, and just as fascinating.

Dog owners come, in time, to resemble their pets. Our research indicates that the same is true of "wet divers" and the marine creatures that are their consuming interest.

So far, our research has been restricted to a handful of branches of the British Sub-Aqua Club. We would be grateful if readers would report sitings of any of the species enumerated below.

THE CLOWN FISH: The precise function of this cheery little fellow in the eco-system has yet to be discovered. But his antics often induce gales of mirth among the other species.

He is best recognised by his behaviour. He is the one who falls out of the boat with no fins on. He regularly forgets to zip up his dry suit before a dive, and is often reminded of the wisdom of turning on his air when he has reached a depth of twenty metres or more.

He is the one whose O-ring blew on the motorway; who sat on the sea urchin; who filled the petrol tank with petrol and two-stroke in the reverse proportions; who drove to St Abbs when the dive was at St Keverne; who dried out the eight-inch artillery shell on the barbecue; who dived with Norman and surfaced with Neville

He is, in short, a berk. There's one in every branch. At least one.

THE COMMON LOBSTER: This sought-after crustacean is

relatively hard to spot at dive sites, preferring the warm, chlorinated waters of the pool. On its rare appearances near salt water, it tends to retreat into corners (eg, between sheets or into sleeping bags) from which it is exceedingly difficult to oust.

The team discovered a large example at Fort Bovisand. Sensing that boats were waiting to be assembled for the morning's diving, it backed into a lower bunk in Dormitory 13 and refused every enticement to emerge. Eventually, it was persuaded to leave its shelter by a crab hook up the nostril. The lobster is covered with a generous layer of soft flesh, and turns bright pink when canned.

THE BORING SPONGE: Like all borers, the sponge gradually eats away at its host until nothing remains. It is usually to be found in the downstairs bar of the *Cat and Hacksaw*, where it drifts in the plankton before attaching itself to a suitable organism. Like many invertebrates, it has no visible means of support, and relies upon its host for sustenance. Only thus can it maintain its fluid levels in a hostile environment.

Occasionally, the host organisms establish a symbiotic relationship with the sponge, wherein its extreme inelasticity (or tightness) is exploited for the benefit of the community (see Treasurer).

THE ECLECTIC HEEL: With its voracious appetite for young flesh, the Heel invariably hunts alone. It lures its victims with promises of large gins while mesmerising them with tales of derring-do at forty metres and swashbuckling adventure on the scallop banks off Lulworth Cove.

It usually selects its prey from the inexperienced ducklings of the branch, who give themselves away by the vivid, blue sheen of their virgin log books. Closing in on its intended victim, it secretes a slick natural oil which charms the duckling into a state of paralysis.

The Heel mates several times in the course of a season.

THE HAMMER-HEAD: What is more awesome than the appetite of this, the prince of sharks? Is there nothing it cannot consume in its solitary, restless patrol beneath the billows? The hammer-head can cause more damage to a wreck in ten minutes than did the catastrophe that sank it.

Our researchers recently landed a monstrous specimen and slit open its goody bag. Inside were three hundredweight of non-ferrous metal, a crystal decanter, two canteens of cutlery, an instrument much favoured by ships' surgeons in Tudor times for the treatment of social diseases, the complete works of Sir Walter Scott, a set of golf clubs, a marble bust of W C Fields, a Yorkshire terrier, part of Skylab, a Louis Quinze flugelhorn, and the internal organs of Lord Lucan.

The hammer-head is easily identified at the dive site. Instead of the usual weight belt, it sports a girdle of lethal ironmongery – wrenches, lump hammers, picks, shovels, Malayan kukris and greasy little wads of nitroglycerine are the stock in trade of this drear scavenger.

COMMON MUSCLE: Closely related to the above is the Common Mussel Man. This species has developed a complex ritual for the attraction (we suppose) of members of the opposite sex. The ritual involves much rippling and strutting, punctuated by feats of prodigious strength. One specimen was observed staggering up Chesil Beach with a 60 horsepower engine under each arm.

When provoked (as with the hoots and jeers of his detractors), *Muscle vulgari* becomes aggressive and will often vent its anger by kicking sand in the faces of nine stone weaklings and by drinking lager without opening the can.

However, its behaviour can be turned, with skilful manipulation, to the advantage of its fellows. It has been known, for instance, to pack the Branch van single-handed while the other species relax in the pub, in the vain hope of winning the approval of some bored and indifferent female.

THE DAB HAND: In stark contrast, the Dab Hand keeps a very low profile at van-loading time. His chief predator is the Dive

Marshal, who pursues him relentlessly around the dive site. However, the Dab is a master of disguise. He lies flat on the sand and adopts the colouring of his surroundings. This makes him invisible to all but the most practised eye.

The above, of course, represents but a tiny proportion of the myriad species inhabiting our shores. Nevertheless, we hope it will inspire new dry divers to continue the work of seeking out and cataloguing these fascinating creatures.

Meanwhile, we prepare eagerly for the coming Winter season, with a full calendar already composed. January sees the start of our pool sessions. (Bring your own cue). The marine identification course commences in February with a field trip to Wheeler's Restaurant in Mayfair. And in March, a group of dry divers with a special interest in the location of old wrecks will be trying to find Michael Foot on Hampstead Heath.

Until next year, then, it's not so much "au reservoir" as "arid vidercci". Goodbye, and stay dry!

CHAPTER 10: *A chilling brush with hypothermia*

Ice cold in Whitechapel

There are moments during the epic motion picture we call Life when the film breaks; when time is frozen and we are allowed to inspect a particular frame in rare and astonishing detail. Was it not James Joyce who dubbed such flashes "epiphanies"?

Well, I experienced an epiphany this morning. There I was in my shorts with the professor and the man in the bath with the headphones on and the terminals attached to his body, listening to Radio 1 as the pumps pushed the luke-warm water through the spaghetti of little white tubes, when suddenly, *epiph!*

The scenario, to the casual on-looker, might have recalled a tableau from *Doctor Gorzo's House of Fear* (1937). In fact, it was a routine day in Professor Keatinge's hypothermia experiment. For here, in this abandoned bath room in the bowels of the London Hospital, the professor has been quietly investigating the human body's response to immersion in cold water – so successfully identifying the mechanisms that operate in low temperatures that many hundreds of divers have cause to bless him silently each morning as they don their woolly bears.

Keatinge did not discover hypothermia. Its effects became all too familiar during the Second World War, when 30 000 men perished as a direct result of their immersion in Arctic waters. Safety equipment was designed to prevent drowning, but not heat loss. Hypothermia (officially described as the state of the body when its core temperature drops below 35° Centigrade) is easily recognisable in a subject on the surface. He complains of cold, then descends into a spiral of predictable symptoms until unconsciousness and death occur.

Keatinge was intrigued by reports of unexplained deaths and instances of confusion and unconsciousness which abounded in the diving industry during the early seventies. In such cases, there were no complaints of thermal discomfort – even though the divers concerned were in full communication with their supervisors. Experts were baffled. It was Professor Keatinge who identified the real culprit as cold.

"In the diving industry of that time, there did not exist a full appreciation of the importance of thermal comfort," he recalls. "For one thing, diver training concentrated on persuading men to carry on *despite* cold. The image of diving did not encourage divers to complain. It was made to seem trivial – a minor discomfort."

Moreover, there were serious problems in maintaining a proper control over the temperature of divers working three and four hundred feet beneath the surface of the sea. Traditionally, commercial divers are kept warm by hot water pumped down from a boiler in the support vessel to the bell, then out via an umbilical to the diver, where it is flushed around the inside of his suit. There exists no independent monitoring system to check the temperature of the water as it reaches the diver.

During a three-week field study in the North Sea in 1979, Keatinge made some significant discoveries. First, he made the first-ever measurements of divers' temperatures as they finished their shifts. "We discovered that 25 per cent of divers tested were at the brink of hypothermia," he recalls.

The professor also made some vital practical observations. He found that it was standard working procedure for a diver to continue working for up to one hour after his heating system had broken down.

Deeper investigation of the hypothermic state revealed certain critical effects on the mental state of the victim. "We discovered that a hypothermic diver loses his ability to memorise. He can still recall old memories – things he learned before he grew cold – but he cannot commit any new information to memory. Also, hypothermia would seem to have a marked effect upon the speed of reasoning. Clearly, both of these effects could have very serious implications in the dangerous working conditions encountered by the diver."

But Professsor Keatinge's most sinister discovery was this: that a body which is uniformly immersed in *luke warm* water is in extreme danger of slipping into the potentially fatal hypothermic state.

To give the diving industry its due, it reacted promptly and with genuine concern to Professor Keatinge's findings. The one-hour "work on" practice was abandoned. Now, a diver is brought in immediately if his heating system malfunctions. In general, far greater importance has been attached to the thermal comfort of divers than was the case before the professor's research.

Meanwhile, Professor Keatinge is continuing his research into the problem of cold in commercial diving. He is currently testing a new heating system, which should solve most of the problems associated with the traditional shipboard boiler method. The diver will carry a small immersion heater on his back, which will circulate warm water through small-bore tubes, sewn into a special under-suit. Most importantly, it will adjust temperature quickly and simply, so that the diver is always working in conditions of maximum thermal comfort.

It was this peculiar and futuristic under-suit which the man in the bath with the headphones was testing. The headphones contained a highly-accurate ear thermometer which measured his temperature. The terminals allowed a continuous read-out of his skin temperature. A pair of off-set pumps provided a flow of water through the tubes of his suit. I was wearing shorts because I'm mildly eccentric.

I became aware of an icy trickle between the toes of my right foot. A rivulet of water was leaking from a waste pipe straight into the ventilation holes of my *Nike Odyssey* training shoes. Within seconds, my ability to reason was noticeably impaired. I was unable to memorise the scene before me. I was becoming sluggish. My surroundings were invested with a strange, dream-like quality.

It seemed to me that I was being addressed from the other side of the universe by a choir of identical professors. Things could have taken a very nasty turn indeed. I was losing heat rapidly through my knees. My Ron Hill shorts were providing less-than-satisfactory thermal protection. If only I could reach the Whitechapel Road before my motor system went, I could flag down a passing ambulance. With any luck, they could get me to the snug of the *Cat and Hacksaw* before I slipped irretrievably into the abyss of unconsciousness.

"I *will,*" I told myself. "I will, I will, I *WILL. . . .*"

Seven days before the mast

Hands up everyone who has dived An-t Lasgair. Nobody? Perfect. I have. It's a desolate, guano-streaked crag off the Isle of Skye.

Its name is Gaelic. It means, "desolate, guano-streaked crag off the Isle of Skye". Gaelic is an amazing language. It sounds as if it was invented by a gang of granite gnomes.

Ant-t Lasgair is one of the remoter places I visited on a whirlwind tour of the Inner Hebrides. Places as uninhabitable, generally, as they are unpronounceable.

The trip was organised by Gordon Ridley, who chartered a magnificent ocean-going trawler for the entire summer. This turns out to have been an inspired gambit. Despite the wind and the fog, the trip afforded good company, a substantial degree of comfort, and scintillating diving – all for the price of a *pina colada* at Stringfellow's.

Here follow edited highlights:

SITE AND DATE: Sligneach Mor (north shore of Loch Sunart), June 21. Bottom time and maximum depth: 23 mins, 28m. Dive details: Probably the most spectacular dive I've ever made in UK waters. Vertical cliff falls away from 2m to 34m. The wall is covered with the most astonishing profusion of life. Trees of orange hard coral, up to six inches in height; tiny transparent tunicates with vivid white tips; massive, pomander-like spheres of sea squirts; grey shelves of soft corals, gigantic plumose anenomes, and a nine-inch bag of disgusting grey-green jelly with lumps in it.

The *Jean de la Lune* is a wonderful boat because it has a shower that works. It has a brace of toilets, and, as everybody knows, two heads are better than one. It has a saloon that is snugger than the snug of the *Rover's Return* with lots of drink in it. The bunks are spacious as bunks go. The cabins have radiators you can turn on *and* off, so you can dry your drawers by day without evaporating by night. She's warm, comfortable and fast. Sail and engine in harness can produce twelve knots. And with Decca Navigator, echo sounder and magnetometer, she makes a highly-sophisticated diving platform. She has a skipper who is skillful, reasonable, and sympathetic to the special needs of a diving payload. But most of all, she is a fine and graceful ship. You walk very tall in Tobermory if you've just come ashore from the *Jean de la Lune*.

THE LAST time I wore my drysuit, I was wading up to my armpits in the primaeval slime of the River Stour. As I kit up, people step involuntarily backwards. Poisonous airs creep from my suit along the deck. I had smelled this sour and sickly odour before, slithering out from the malarial swamps of the Skeleton Coast. But that's another story . . .

SITE AND DATE: Calve Island, Tobermory, June 21. Bottom time and maximum depth: 13 minutes, 28m. Dive details: Another fabulous dive. Ten metres from shore, the bottom falls away in a sheer cliff. Skipper reads the depth here as 70m. The walls are thick with 12cm Sea Squirts (Cerianthus Lloydi). Some interesting soft corals and Devonshire cup corals, but really the most impressive feature of the site is the sheer scale of the drop-off. Saw another horrible bag of rotting jelly. These unspeakable things will haunt me to the grave.

CRUISED OUT of Tobermory (Isle of Mull) at dawn. That's about midnight in these rarified latitudes. Staggered on deck in a heavy swell. Gordon R. writes in his notes that a rolling ship is a sure sign of seaworthiness. In which case, *Jean de la Lune* is a safer bet at Lloyds than Noah's Ark.

Pouring the morning cuppa was like a game in *It's A Knockout*. After a hearty breakfast, we retired to the after-deck and amused ourselves with a projectile vomiting competition.

Then the sails went up. Instantly, *Jean* heeled to a modest six degrees, and carved a rock-steady swathe through the foaming main.

WE EXCHANGE "descend" signals, Jeremy Caravick and I, outside a cave in a wall of granite.

The cave waits black and tense like the mouth of a cat.

Needless to say, I attempt to descend with my snorkel in my mouth instead of my DV. At the surface again, using only the line from an ordinary SMB, I execute my famous impression of spaghetti on a fork.

When I finally join Jeremy at ten metres, he is asleep.

Gingerly we walk in the shadow of the valley of death. Within the cliff, there is no light and no life.

Jeremy motions me to turn off my torch. Ahead, a ghostly incandescence. Turning a corner, the water is suddenly shot with shafts of silver. They flicker and dance like the projectionist's beam in a silent cinema.

The surface parts to reveal the roof of a cave like a cathedral. Through an organ-pipe fissure floods fog-soaked light which plays a glittering fugue upon the myriad facets of the rock.

It is one of those trapped-in-amber moments we all dive for. After all, if I seriously believed it was all going to be Stoney Cove in March, a stirred-up bottom, and one 2nd Class to every twenty E&F's, I'd sew up the seals on my drysuit and grow herbs in it.

A WORD about Our Hostess. Kaye Burton is unarguably the most competent human on the planet. She has apparently dispensed with the need for sleep. She remains breezy in a Force 7 while cooking for fifteen in a galley the size of an Austin Metro, and pitched at 30 degrees to boot.

Unbidden, she will dash out to the deck in her apron, scamper up the rigging like a flying squirrel, and perform incredible feats of dexterity with wildly-lashing lines.

Between substantial, satisfying meals, she will spirit up endless jugs of tea and coffee. She can tie a Turk's Head. She effortlessly achieves the perfect balance between friendliness and professional detachment, and she makes the *Jean de la Lune* a very special dive boat indeed.

IN PORTREE, the beer is called "Seventy Bob". At *The Cat And Hacksaw*, the Branch speakeasy, seventy shillings is roughly the price of a pint. Not so in Portree, where you can drink yourself to death for the price of a copy of *Diver*.

HOW I SHALL miss Uig. The expression of childlike trust and innocence on the faces of the natives as they try to run us down in their 'N' registered Allegros is one I will cherish forever.

As that quaint little port shrinks in our wake, the fog

grudgingly moves over to make room for the heavy rain and high winds which have been queuing up to assault us since Saturday. The storm clouds boil over the gloomy crags of Ben Trumùn and foam upon the raging tides of Arthurscar Gill.

We find a bicycle in the forward locker and devise a new distraction: someone puts Wagner's Meistersingers on the stereo and the rider has to pedal round the deck before Side 1 ends. The record so far is 4 hrs 27 mins.

DIVING WITH underwater photographers can be tedious. Rather like dancing a rumba with Douglas Bader.

I would offer this thought only: if you set your focus to Infinity and your shutter speed to Eternity, would you get a photograph of God?

SITE AND DATE: Canna, June 25. Bottom time and maximum depth: 25 minutes, 25m. Dive details: Off rocks near island. Dozens of squat lobsters (munida rugosa?) and different varieties of starfish. One we measure as 17 inches in diameter. Everything here is enormous. Feather stars, each feather six inches long; huge kelp plants at 12m with sail-like wings, 3m by 2m; scallops like frisbees; huge colonies of "light bulb" tunicates. My buddy knifes an urchin and offers the best bits to a massive wrasse. It stares at him as if he were mad, and swaggers insolently away into the gloom.

I'VE BEEN AROUND, believe me. I've dived the dizzy 100m wall at Kimmeridge. I've plumbed the abyssal plains of Northam Pit. I've sported with sperm whales at Henley-on-Thames and discovered whole new species of thorn-backed rays off Great Yarmouth.

The Inner Hebrides makes monkeys of them all.

The sea there is a living lesson in conservation. Once, before the chlorides and the benzoles and the filthy isotopes of heavy metals with their built-in legacy of 20 000 gene-curdling years, the English Channel and the Irish Sea must have bloomed with the same rich harvest as the waters of the Western Isles. My advice is this: dive them while you can, then write it all down before the memory fades into a dream.

CHAPTER 12: *The ups and downs of wreck location*

On your marks!

"Who knows the marks?"

"Neville knows the marks."

"I don't. I never said I did."

"You did. I bloody well heard you. You distinctly said, 'I know the marks'."

"I might conceivably have implied that I knew *one* of the marks. Approximately."

"That's not the impression you gave. You made out you knew precisely where the marks were."

"Gentlemen, gentlemen. We've been at sea for 50 minutes, it's practically dark, the plowman homeward plods his weary way, et cetera. The bar's open. My wetsuit is infested by a colony of termites with herpes. And you're still arguing about the marks."

"Who's arguing? I never claimed to know . . ."

"You did! You did!"

"Didn't."

"DID! DID! DID!"

"Alright. It's the tree."

"What?"

"The mark is the tree."

"Listen, limpet-brain: we're fifty yards from the biggest forestry plantation in Northern Europe, and you're talking about a tree.

"It's the tree that's *different*."

"What do you mean, different?"

"Different. Not the same. Distinct. Unusual. Atypical. Contrary to your general trend, tree-wise.

"Neville, I ask this merely out of scientific curiosity: have

you ever eaten a flare?"

Familiar? The Great Marks Squabble. Who really does know the marks? The transits? The precious, ineluctable coordinates?

There's a cox in our branch who exudes the quiet authority of the master navigator. His jaw set square to the wind, he braces himself between the stringers of an inflatable like Apollo bestride his sun chariot.

Let us call him Colin.

Suddenly, he will throttle back. With quick and expert eye, he scans the shore. "Kit up," he mutters. "We're there." Then: "Do you want the stern or the foc'sle?"

Nobody has anticipated the luxury of a choice. "Well . . . er . . . whatever . . ."

"OK. Now, when I say go, you've got to go. Otherwise, you'll drift way off. I'm putting you into twenty-three metres. Maybe twenty-four. Go!"

And sure enough . . . we drop neatly into 18ft of gloomy, impenetrable kelp. In 40 minutes of sightless floundering about, we encounter a platoon of periwinkles and a solitary, moronic blenny.

Colin, you see, couldn't land a kite on Africa.

He is directionally dyslexic. He wears a compass, but it might as well be made of marzipan. Like so many poor sailors on this brief and stormy passage round the Cape of Life, Colin sports a flimsy oilskin of competence. But underneath, he is a far-from-able seaman – a kind of involuntary nomad, doomed to tread the trackless, watery wastes until eternity.

All the more amazing that we should once have elected him Diving Officer.

Still, that's the lovable old BS-AC in a seashell. You'd have to arrange a dive in Sainsbury's carpark, Cheam, before anyone so much as raised an eyebrow.

Even now, the future is not all gloom for Colin. He has proved himself so brilliant at avoiding wrecks that the Tees and Hartlepool Port Authority has offered him a pilot's ticket.

Not that my own track record is significantly better.

Once, quite accidentally, I dropped four divers bang on to a wreck near the Bovisand Shagstone. I managed to disguise my astonishment when they surfaced with the news. I even feigned mild boredom: "Oh, really? Oh, my! Won't you just look at that sunset!" Back in the bar, I was practically canonised.

Nowadays, of course, I never miss a wreck. I have developed a foolproof system which makes sonar look like water devining. I was planning to sell the idea to NATO. But instead, Gentle Reader, I'll share it with you.

Rule One: Never rise before ten am on the morning of the dive. A generous breakfast, a desultory flick through the world's press, then a stroll down to the dive site. On no account should the first boat be in the water before noon.

One should then summon a native – some quaint, ethnic fisher-person. "My man!" you must exclaim, "Any notion of the whereabouts of one *James Egan Layne*?"

"Arr-r-rh!", the person will saltily reply. "The ol' Jay Eee Layne? Steer 232 degrees Nor-Nor-West, young zur, an' there be she!"

"Is that left or right?" you inquire.

And so on. In the end, you will merely put to sea and drive. When roughly half an hour has elapsed, one of your divers will remark: "There are six inflatables over there. Just to the right of the pointed end."

"Ah good!" you will reply with real satisfaction. For where six inflatables are gathered together, there, without a shadow of a doubt, is your wreck.

Simple? Certainly. But then all the best ideas are.

CHAPTER 13: *Exotic dives around a fiery isle*

The Lanzarote connection

Perhaps the most interesting thing about Lanzarote is that it has no connection whatsoever with the planet Earth. Britannia Airways is actually a cover for a fleet of interstellar warp modules, flitting across the void of space to far-flung outposts of our galaxy.

Inland, Lanzarote looks like the dark-side of the moon. Great oceans of lifeless lava lap against volcanoes which spit intermittent spumes of steam into the arid blue sky above.

Occasional camels sway on far ridges: a bizarre suggestion of *Beau Geste Meets Dan Dare.*

Down on the East Coast, the Spaniards have done a slightly better job of synthesising a Terran landscape. The shore is craggy. Meandering groins of magma stand petrified where, 130 years ago, they spluttered white-hot into the Atlantic from the erupting cone of Monte del Fuego.

Odd, then, to bump into Bob Wright from Swanage. He runs the Clubulanza diving centre at Puerto del Carmen. Bob is a long-term exile who has traded the sombre pleasures of Dorset diving for the sun-soaked waters of the Saharan coast.

The club nestles in a sheltered corner of the port and is built in the predominant architectural style of the island – a sort of Senior Lego daubed with sugar icing.

Bob runs the show with a laconic, Brit version of *manana* – not inefficiency, more a supreme economy of effort. The vital things get done. The hire-gear is in peak condition; the bottles are blown by a noisy open-air compressor that is probably audible in Tangiers; the beer is always cold.

Ninety per cent of Bob's diving is from his own foreshore. A flight of steps drops down to the sea from a changing area

complete with rinse tank and barbecue.

The ocean at Puerto del Carmen is like the Med with tides – an important plus in the light of the disastrous pollution now afflicting that once-great diving environment.

A virile swell swishes about the steps, and getting into the sea can be tricky, mid-tide in full equipment. Once in, though, the water is deliciously refreshing – seventy degrees in December and varying little throughout the year.

My buddy was Tony Chapman, of BS-AC West Wickham. He and I dived in longjohns and jackets – more for protection against stings and spines than for insulation.

A 200m snorkel took us to the first reef – a rocky terrace on a 20-degree slope from shore to the 3000m abyss of the open sea. The reef is clearly visible from the surface – the next best thing to the Second Coming to anyone who, like me, has mislaid his buddy in 5m of freezing Whitby silt.

Speaking as critically as I can, Lanzarote could do with a

branch or two of coral. The warm, sheltered water with its convenient rocky outcrops should provide a perfect environment for coral, were it not for the recent volcanic activity. Volcanic dust goes down like a lead balloon with coral, and it takes hundreds of years before polyps will establish themselves firmly on igneous rock.

Still, the spartan lava ridges have their compensations. The reefs are a constant source of spectacular cliffs and caves, for the rock is young and still sternly resistant to the mellowing influence of erosion.

We would climb a range of 'foothills', luminescent in the vivid turquoise water, to find ourselves suddenly on the brink of a breathtaking drop. There, from a razor-like ridge, the rock would fall off into dizzy depths so profound that a seasoned mountaineer could not have suppressed a shudder of vertigo.

In terms of density, the amount of observable marine life in Lanzarote is not great. This is typical of most sub-tropical waters. It is only on coral reefs that the number of distinct living organisms can match that to be found in the English Channel.

But the animals here are often individually more spectacular than our own. It is quite common, for instance, to discover in a secluded cave a shoal of tiny golden fry, glittering in torchlight like a rain of living fire. Or to watch the graceful, gladiatorial dance of a stick-like arrow crab with a twelve-inch brittle star. Or to catch backward dagger-glances from a brace of squid as they change down into reverse hyperdrive for a dart-like getaway.

The ocean floor is littered with the shells of exotic molluscs – a constant temptation to jackdaw conchologists like myself, although the small print on the Spanish diving permit forbids the removal of anything, living or dead, from the water. Nevertheless, I did find some small colonies of true coral as well as some stoical representatives of the soft coral *Pennatulacea.*

In the south of the island, at the foot of Fire Mountain, lies the little fishing port of Playa Blanca. One day during our stay, Tony and I stacked our hired Seats to the rafters with Clubulanza bottles and whined our way down to sample the diving at an isolated spot just 5km south of the town.

The rocky foreshore in the Playa Blanca area quickly vanishes beneath a submarine wadi of Saharan sand, so our dives were necessarily shallow. Personally, I have never subscribed to the bet-you-can't-dive-as-deep-as-I-do school. And, at 6m, we enjoyed the full richness of natural colour while spinning out our 60 cu ft bottles almost to eternity.

In the lea of Lanzarote's southern-most peninsula, the water was still and rich with life. Five small barracuda flashed past as we hit bottom (but how small must a barracuda be before you dare call him chicken?).

Finding an especially big and dozy sea cucumber, I exploited him to make a lewd gesture at my buddy. In a split instant, the vile brute had trussed me like a mummy in strands of sticky silk. One of the most effective martial arts ever to destroy a £100 wetsuit.

Then there was the vivid little catapillar, all reds and yellows and fluffy with it, the little love. I captured his two diminutive inches in a clenched fist and hurried after Tony, childishly intent on showing him my prize.

The swine stung me.

Minutes after I'd thoughtfully returned him to a comfortable cranny, my hand contracted into blazing paralysis. It felt as if it had been captured by the Inquisition, plunged into a nest of man-eating hornets, bound in stinging nettles, rinsed in molten lead, severed at the wrist, and tossed to a pack of rabid dobermans.

Consumed by an exquisite agony, I proffered the throbbing hand to Tony. Smiling broadly, he shook it. It is at such times that the diver's code of submarine signals seems woefully inadequate.

Early next morning we got roped into the Old Buoy Network. A portly soft furnishings tycoon from Salford had us trying to free the anchor of his floating gin palace. The chain had jammed on a reef at 20m. Not a great dive. It's amazing what people chuck off moored yachts: there was enough rusty metal on the bottom to build a Lancia Beta.

Mildly hungover, I was still haunted by a persistent dream of the previous night. (Anthony Quinn bequeathed me the Spitfire he keeps in a hangar near Salonika). I was caught off-guard by a spiny urchin. Once embedded in human flesh, its vicious calcinareous barbs are irremoveable, save by a digital version of open heart surgery. I may never play the viola again.

I'm a veteran of the Red Sea where the wildlife is unionised into terror squads, hell-bent on slaughtering tourists. Miraculously, I escaped from Eilat without serious injury. But I shall probably be shipped home from Lanzarote on three separate flights, the subject of some epic jigsaw job at Papworth Hospital. Gentlemen, we have the technology.

The final dive, happily, was our best. We snorkelled for an age, then finally sank in the lea of a ghastly pink schooner registered in Poole and crewed by a select committee of the Monday Club, the members of which probably made their fortunes selling polythene ballarinas in Dubai.

I was momentarily alarmed to find my depth gauge registering 35m, but I'd encountered worse visibility in Clapham Baths. For fifteen gloriously-extruded minutes we soared across the facets of an imperial reef. A squadron of angel fish executed a fly-past of breathless, silvery precision. Wonderful, massive oyster shells leapt from the sea-floor into my cupped palms, and a platoon of nudibranchia staged a waltz-time tattoo – touching in its ambling innocence. Meanwhile, Tony blasted off so many flash cubes that his Olympus went all malleable and the very rocks reeled under a barrage of electronic artillery.

Fourteen days were too few.

I could have learned windsurfing – Christiana's school offers a seven-day course, the hours of which slot neatly between dives at Clubulanza.

I could have joined the Berlin Brigade at the German Tauchschule for formation snorkelling and platinum-plated demand valves, burnishing of.

I could even have tampered with delicious Lanzarote nubettes in secluded reaches of the Joker discotheque.

But I didn't. I basked in 85 degrees of December sunshine, drank far too much Sangria, and ate so much octopus that Davy Jones' Locker is probably a sitting duck for pilferers.

I shot three 35mm films that will leave Lord Lichfield apoplectic with envy. I was especially proud of one snap. It might have been snatched by Mariner VII during a micro-second's dash past Saturn. Lanzarote; a barren cinder beneath a merciless, alien sun.

Back in London, I showed it to a diving acquaintance of mine who runs a solid fuel business.

"With what you paid for yer 'oliday," he said, "I could 'ave delivered the 'ole bloody island at yer 'ouse in sacks."

CHAPTER 14: *Christmas diving in Central London*

The slimy secrets of the Serpentine

Christmas Day: while anyone with a sense of occasion sprawled comatose in front of *Ben Hur,* the rugged pioneers of London BS-AC were kitting up. Above them, leaden skies. Beside them, the unplumbed depths of a chill, British man-made lake.

Conversation was limited to grunted expletives. Each diver was lost in a world of private apprehensions: for a great question-mark hung over this desolate place.

What lay beneath that oily calm? . . . An endless, midnight spiral into an abyss, leagues beyond the bounds of our imaginings? The spiny populace of nightmare-blind-eyed and needle-toothed creatures in the slime of the centuries?

On the horizon, mist-enshrouded and enigmatic, towered the British Gas building in Seymour Street.

Thirteen men and one woman finally surrendered themselves to the icy coils of London's Serpentine.

How could they have known they were only minutes away from the most sensational submarine discovery since the *Mary Rose* – a 1953 Ford Popular, perfectly preserved in the primaeval mud of Hyde Park?

The car turned out to be a veritable time-capsule, a fascinating glimpse into the lives of our ancestors. A small adjustable wrench, charming in its simplicity; a boiled sweet; a copy of *Health and Efficiency,* still quite unreadable after all these years.

The Popular has since been designated a preservation area. When eventually raised, she is to be restored and part-exchanged for a new Branch Training Officer.

The Serpentine is supplied by all that remains of the Bay, one of London's lost rivers. For more than a hundred years, visitors to Hyde Park have gaily tossed their rubbish, their small change, their valuables and (as it turns out) their Ford Populars into it's murky depths.

This fact had not escaped Simon Mordant – a Third Class diver but first class criminal brain. It was he who put together the most bloodcurdling team of pirates since Blackbeard's. It was he who duped the Department of the Environment into granting official permission for the expedition. It was he who logged the longest dive of all – 55 minutes in 3m of olive-coloured crushed ice.

And it was he who answered the burning question of the day. Was there any visible life in the Serpentine? Yes, in a sense! There was visible death, anyway, in the shape of two, large, deceased fish. There was also a perch in a bottle. There was no weed. But then, there wouldn't be: it was December, after all, and weed is seasonal.

Simon found a brass cashbox, dating from the turn of the century. The lock was drilled, so the box was obviously chucked from the bridge by its wrongful owner.

Other finds included dozens of dinner plates, scores of mesh wastepaper baskets (Louis XIV?), tons of masonry from the bridge, billions of Coke cans, and what Simon proudly describes as "a big white jug, enamel".

But it was Branch Jackdaw Paul Watts who risked his all in an arm's length of duck droppings to rescue an Aladdin's cave of ancient bottles. For the benefit of bottle freaks, the rarer specimens included a 19th century stone jam-jar; an R. White's stone bottle dating back to the 1850s; a Codd mineral-water bottle complete with marble and inscribed "H. Valentine, Clapham"; and another marked "Hooper Struve, Established 1825". This latter carries the words "By Appointment" and the royal coat of arms.

Sceptical police frogmen (why are police divers always called "frogmen"?) predicted nil visibility for the dive. But in fact it was occasionally as good as 1.5m. Hardly the Red Sea, but not bad for central London in December.

At any rate, Simon and his band of cockleshell heroes were quite undaunted by the experience and are now poised for a further assault on the secrets of the Serpentine.

Me, I'm eagerly looking forward to *Ben Hur II*.

CHAPTER 15: *Underwater explosives for beginners*

Light the blue touch-paper . . .

The Date: 1981. The Place: The top secret HQ of Major "Mad" Bill Britton's infamous phantom squad. The mission: To bend a bit of rusty pipe in six metres of untreated effluent near Plymouth.

It was Wednesday, I recall. I woke with a dim recollection of having given money to somebody at the *Perseverance*, a Marylebone hostelry much favoured by Our Lot. My worst suspicions were soon confirmed. I had agreed to join four branch members on the Bovisand explosives course. Worse, I had actually paid for the privilege. May the Saints preserve us from India Pale Ale and all the foolishness therein.

The course was subsequently postponed because of bad weather. (Privately I thought a brisk Force Ten would have added to the fun. What could be finer than to sit on the bottom of Bovisand harbour in nil visibility and a gravel-lined wetsuit, fumbling with a mit-full of lethal detonators in a typhoon, after all?) We were finally rescheduled for May and dutifully pitched up at the Fort for an early Saturday start.

The grown-ups on the Advanced course went off to sink Russian trawlers with Exocet missiles. The rest of us filed down into the bowels of the building to meet our instructor. On the door of our classroom was posted a photograph of a hospital cot containing a mound of ragged flesh. The caption read: "Four into one *will* go!"

Bill was our boy. He'd been making explosions for twenty-five years and was still reasonably intact. A good omen. He is of Albion's best. The sort who could win an Empire with one hand tied behind his back, then lose it again with one gloriously irresponsible act of Great British gallantry.

I imagined us in that very bunker during the Last Show in '41 – four perfect specimens of rugged soldiery, quietly awaiting our final briefing from Major "Mad" Bill Britton, legendary commander of the Phantom Squad.

Mad Bill: At ease gentlemen. You may smoke. Now . . . (stabs at chart with rusty bayonet) . . this is Peenemunde, the Jerries' top secret rocket base. And this . . . is Allied Command, Fort Bovisand. I spoke to Winnie this morning. 'Bill', he says, 'give me Peenemunde!'

'By heaven, Prime Minister,' I said, 'give me Blackford and four good men and I'll bring it to you in a bottle!'

We kicked off with a general chat on explosives. Low explosive fuses of the "light blue touch-paper and retire" variety, and the awesome high explosive type which "burns" at a rate of 9000 metres per second.

We learned how to crimp detonators on to the ends of fuses. (There's enough RDX in a standard detonator to take your hand off at the wrist. It's about as stable as an Italian government). We gawked at one-inch steel plates split like toffee bars by modest charges of gelignite. We discovered how to string together a dozen chunks of plastic explosive for simultaneous detonation. And we fiddled with electrical firing devices straight out of *Bridge On the River Kwai.* And then we trooped out with a trunk of goodies to the blockhouse just west of the Fort for our first practical session.

This course was beginning to remind me of November 5, 1957. There was essentially no difference between four grown men learning how to atomise a concrete blockhouse and Tony Howitt next door putting bangers in lemonade bottles.

Cordtex fuse looks like plastic-coated washing line. It is packed with HE (high explosive to you non-technical garbage). HE is stable, so it must be detonated before it will explode. We reeled out a few metres of Cordtex and taped on a detonator which, in turn, was to be fired electrically from a respectful distance. We squabbled over who should press the button. I won. I cranked up the machine, blew three blasts on my whistle, and then pushed.

The effect of high explosives is the closest thing to magic I have ever encountered. That so much din and destruction can be unleashed by such a puny, undistinguished lump of mud is quite beyond my comprehension. Cornwall leapt out of its skin on the horizon. All the molecules in everything did a frantic momentary mazurka. I guarantee a survey would reveal a sudden rise in the number of premature births among farm animals within a six-mile radius of the fort. And that was just the fuse.

The hard stuff is something else again. Bill tossed me a half-pound stick and I dropped it. My whole life flashed before my eyes (not a pretty sight) but Bill explained, "HE is stable. You can jump on it, throw it at the wall and it won't explode. You can even burn it".

To prove his point, he set fire to a piece and it burned with a fierce, incandescent flame. One stick of submarine explosive will boil a kettle in 80 seconds. At 40p a stick, it costs about the same as a Zippo firelighter. But whack a detonator on it and it suddenly demands the respect you would accord a rabid tigress.

That afternoon, we demolished a sea wall which had successfully resisted the onslaught of the English Channel for a hundred years.

Next day, we prepared to put our new-found skills to the test. Demolition in the dry was one thing. Attaching charges underwater was another.

In 8m, the visibility was appalling. Gaston (the Branch Frenchman) and I slithered down a line to our chunk of scrap iron selected from the Bovisand tip. In a dry runthrough, we had established where the charges would be set for maximum effect. But binding putty to a rusty spar in a running tide in nil vis can be quite tricky.

Eventually we clambered into our boat and Bill rigged the detonators to the Cordtex lead. These were, in turn, connected to a long cable which ran underwater to the jetty. We signalled to Gary, who manned the plunger. He hit the button. Nothing happened.

We weren't surprised. It hadn't happened for the "B" team's charges either. They'd spent an hour trying to locate the fault, while taking it in turns to chuck up over the side.

The hours dragged by. Sometimes the detonator failed, sometimes the Cordtex. Sometimes everything went off except the charge. And sometimes nothing went off at all. Dusk was chilly. The sea was restless and the air thick with salt spray. We were all tired and discouraged.

The whole scenario reminded me of an illustration from the 1946 *Lion* annual. (Lieutenant Cardew scanned the lights of the arctic convoy ploughing remorselessly North. Caption: "What wouldn't I give for a mug of your cocoa, Bo'sun!")

One more try. Three more blasts on the whistle. Hit the button . . . And there occurred a detonation which shook the very foundations of Bovisand jetty. It must have registered upon seismographs in Irkutsk.

"Zare!" exclaimed a triumphant Gaston. "It is as I sort! We were simply overqualified for ze job!"

And as Mad Bill hurried off to storm an embassy somewhere, the Frenchman threw his arms about our shoulders.

"We men," he said. "Are we not marvellous?"

Fins ain't what they used to be

Call me an old-fashioned patriot if you like, but I can't repress a surge of pride when I see London No. 1 Branch BS-AC right up there at the forefront of the technological revolution, boldly going where no branch has gone before.

There was a time when, to become a diver, all a chap needed was a set of rubber undies, an old fire extinguisher, and a mutated 'y' chromosome. But those days are gone forever. In the underground laboratories, deep underneath No. 1 Branch's Scientific Establishment in Seymour Street, Professors Nicholson and Wray slave endlessly in pursuit of an impossible dream.

Impossible? . . . I am now in a position to reveal that Nicholson and Wray are to be awarded a Nobel Prize for their work in astrophysics, ultrasonics and sub-particle navigation.

At a meeting of the branch's Extra-Terrestial Affairs Committee, Professor Keith Nicholson, before a stunned audience, unveiled the "bottom line" of eight years of research and development. The Satellite-Instigated Navigation Computer (SINC) is probably the most sophisticated piece of electronic processing equipment to come out of the Marble Arch area during the last 6 weeks.

Designed to fit neatly into the club's inflatables – *Bismark, Scharnhost,* and *Tirpitz* – the digital 'brain' is no larger than a small semi-detached bungalow. The operator will, of course, hold a BS-AC Micro Electronics Endorsement, earned at one of the Club's training weekends at the Massachusetts Institute of Technology.

As he tunes the delicate circuitry of the great computer, a needle-fine beam of laser light scans the sky until it locates the

Branch communications satellite, poised in a stable orbit two thousand miles out in the timeless void of space.

Imperceptibly, the satellite's photo-sensors home in on the coordinates of the ground party, their progress registering as a diminishing set of valves on SINC's visual display screen.

So far, the SINC system is of use only in the sphere of subaquatic nutrition. Low frequency noise is beamed down into the sea from the orbiting space module. This causes severe depression among neurotically-inclined scallops, which then give themselves up to any diver wearing the insignia of the London No. 1 Branch Crustacean Recovery Agency. However, once the Club Fleet has been refitted with nuclear propulsion units, SINC's applications will proliferate endlessly.

Professors Nicholson and Wray are already working on a computerised nautical teasmade, a laser-fired lobster irritator and a remote-controlled rubber duck for the bored coxswain.

Is there no end to the ingenuity of these frontiersmen in the field of human advancement? No limit to their almost visionary perception of the diver's Destiny?

I suspect not.

NEXT WEEK: First Class Diver-Philosopher Sigmund Sisman re-examines Kant's Analytic in the light of new advances in snorkel design.

Getting the site right

It's midnight in Maida Vale. The crumbling mansions of a once-fashionable Edwardian crescent are sunk in the bloodless sleep of the very old.

The silence is broken only by a low electrical hum which emanates from a workshop concealed behind the flaking facade. Tonight, as on countless similar nights, a handful of dedicated technicians slave ceaselessly to achieve the impossible – coaxing, tuning, improvising, tweaking and cajoling their antiquated equipment into another weekend's reluctant service.

Lo! By Friday the miracle is complete. The equipment is crammed into the club transport (itself a monument to the inventors of pop rivets and gaffer tape), and London Branch BS-AC is on the road again. Mobile and operational.

As we roll slowly out of town towards the unplumbed depths of the Atlantic, the Marshal runs through a mental checklist: nearest Coastguard, recompression facilities, telephone. *Check.* Tide times and flows. *Check.* Availability of Wadworth's 6X. *Check.*

Compared to the organisational complexities of a weekend in Devon, the Trans Globe Expedition is like nipping down to the corner shop for a packet of fags.

As rosy-fingered dawn first caresses the crags of Burgh Island, the grim commandos of the branch are already in action on the beach.

They toss outboard engines to one another with the effortless ease of Marvel superheroes. They skip lightly down to the water's edge with armfuls of aqualungs. They communicate in a private language of grunts and gasps learned in the great sandwich course of Life's rough university.

The van spews forth its rugged secrets. Flags, flares, buoys, paddles, echo sounders, lines and anchors, props and wrenches, pins, bolts, keels, funnels and tanks. All wrapped in the good, wholesome stink of The Branch at Sea: a tangy amalgam of rubber, brine-and-petrol, toffee-thick marine varnish, and ancient whelks.

The divers arrive. Each the font of very special skills, hammered home in pool and lecture, honed and polished to the keenest edge of competence.

And all their kit. Glittering, pampered darlings, representing months of labour in shops and schools and offices, or anywhere divers must work a week for thirty magic minutes under the sea.

Finally, the boat puts out from Challaborough – bobbing with preposterous optimism upon the brightly-dancing wavelets of the bay.

And around the point she vanishes, bearing the inestimably valuable results of years of training, thousands of pounds of capital investment, and the priceless devotion of everyone concerned – from Caesar's midnight crusaders to the little E&F who helped inflate the Tomos.

As a matter of fact, I was on that boat. I dropped into 12m of water and landed on a sandy bottom of such glorious, all-transcending monotony that for 22 minutes I had to battle against the onset of catatonic trance. Even my three dahlia anenomes (the only life-forms I encountered during the dive) seemed bored and listless.

Surely, they seemed to say, there must be more to life than this?

Now then, South Devon is a long way from London. Quite apart from the combined effort, organisation and expertise required to shift the branch there, it cost me nearly sixty quid in petrol.

Moreover, that particular stretch of coastline offers some of the most spectacular diving in Britain. There are fabulous drop-offs in gin-clear water. There are reefs, gullies and walls galore – all a-sparkle with a fabulous wealth of jewel anemones, feather stars, encrusting sponges, and all the rest of the multifarious submarine junk that festoons the better dive sites of this sceptred isle.

And so it occurred to me forcibly that my dive on to that Saharan terrain was not only an expensive disaster, but also a tragedy of lost opportunities.

Yet I would wager there isn't a member of any BS-AS branch who hasn't experienced a similar disappointment or two with every season.

Heavens! Even amid the exotic wonderworld of the

Manacles, I only managed two dives in three days which I couldn't have experienced in dear old Dorset.

Clearly, something is wrong. We, like many other BS-AC branches, have echo sounders, charts, able and intelligent dive marshals. We organise our diving with superb efficiency. And yet, so often, we are let down at the really critical point in the whole operation – the dive itself.

Why? We have access to guide books and the Wreck Register. We have the naked gall required to tackle the local fishermen. We have the gumption, presumably, to head for a conglomeration of dive boats in the knowledge that 25 other coxwains can't simultaneously be wrong.

The situation at London Branch is, I suspect, typical of many other BS-AC branches up and down the country. And thus I propose that it should become a major priority of all diving clubs to organise the very best diving for members. Not on the grand, macro scale of The Expedition, but on the immediate, tumble-out-of-the-boat-into-paradise level which, after all, is the bottom line of any trip to the coast.

Every branch in Britain should elect someone whose sole responsibility it is to suss out the lie of the water; to quiz coastguards, fishermen, local divers, the Marine Conservation Society, the BS-AC hierarchy; to scan the pages of diving guide books, the Wreck Register, marine biology textbooks, and Folk Legends of Dorset (Vol. XXIV). In short, generally to make sure that when a British diver flops into the ocean he is automatically bound, hell-for-neoprene, for adventure among stunning panoramas of super-natural beauty, or rare, archaeological treats that make the *Mary Rose* look like a plastic duck in a baby's bath.

CHAPTER 18: *Diving, running, and the fitness freaks*

Smash the yoga nancy boys!

Anybody who, like me, has been forced to take off his depth-gauge before hauling himself over the side of the inflatable, must recognise the value of a little physical fitness.

But with all due respect, I think that *Diver*, in its recent articles on physical fitness*, has been guilty of a fundamental misapprehension about the psychology of your average BS-AC member.

Own up, Bern. Yoga's very London NW1. It's part of the Aware Lifestyle. The stipped-pine-and-brown-rice lot does yoga.

The no make-up, long-straight-greasy-hair, Beatrix Potter weave-your-own-children, I'm-not-a-Christian-but-I-have-my-own-personal-vision-of-God merchants do a quick spot of Life Force Inhalation before dropping Emily and Storm at the Nihilist Kids' Co-operative and going to the Chalk Farm Gentle Foods Boutique for this week's ferkin of slippery elm roughage supplement.

Most divers drink twelve pints of unreal ale before lunch. They don't feel as if they've eaten a proper meal until they've torn the flesh off living beast and washed it down with a pint of Daddy's Favourite.

The out-of-London boys I've dived with think marine conservation is something you do to a brass porthole with a pipe hammer and a monkey wrench. When their club van breaks down on the M3, they eat it and make a new one out of old refrigerators.

For instance: I'd really have to pick my moment before I tried teaching Rishi's Posture to Whitby Branch.

And I can just picture the lads from Kendal, half way up Great Gable in a blizzard and full equipment, doing Alternative

Side Bends before this week's night dive in a frozen radioactive tarn.

No. There must be a more suitable way for divers to lose a little weight, gain a little muscle tone, and make at least a token stand against the ravages of Red Barrel and Capstan Full Strength.

The answer, friends, is *running.*

Notice I don't say *jogging.* Jogging is what non-runners call running. Jogging is as much a part of Hampstead Man as yoga and macrobiotic diets. Jogging involves vast monthly expenditure on gas-loaded orthotic footwear, guaranteed whale-free by Greenpeace. And slick poolside track-suits from Harrods (Dry Clean Annually Then Air Between Mink).

Recently, I accidentally entered the Shaston Gold Rush – a three-mile race from the top of Shaftesbury Hill down to the plain and back up to town. The last 500m are up Gold Hill – famous for Hovis ads and the gruelling Fanny-dies-of-consumption scene in *Far from the Madding Crowd.*

Out of a field of 90, I came sixteenth. Then – wait for it – I ran the four miles to a friend's cottage at Cann.

A year ago this Herculean feat would have killed me. But over the months I've added to the daily dose until I could easily manage the current hour-a-day regime.

I like running because it's mindless. After a couple of weeks it ceases to hurt. Your brain idles in a semi-hypnotic state. You become childishly fond of children, birds, squirrels and butterflies. You notice details like: they haven't cleaned the '68 Rover outside Number 12 for at least three days; and my, the Robinsons' little girl is certainly growing up quickly.

Apply the principle in Dorset (last Kimmeridge dive, I ran from the harbour up the Ridgeway and back in 45 minutes), and it becomes Sightseeing for the Man in a Hurry.

My running buddy in Sturminster Newton regularly does a 35-mile jaunt which takes in Okeford Hill, Bulbarrow, Hambledon and Hod Hills, and Spreadeagle. During the run, he sees five English counties and more wildlife than you and I would see in a year if we didn't dive.

At the end of the day, his heart and lungs are strengthened, his blood oxygenated, his chest expanded, his aggression burned off, and his muscles honed to the peak of perfection. And he can settle down to drinking himself into the gutter with a clear conscience.

Next May I'm running in the London Marathon, as well as at least one other 26-mile trot in Portsmouth.

I've already started training. If anybody would like to join me, I'll always do a stint in Hyde Park before pool sessions.

And because I always run 'aerobically', you should have enough breath left to curse me all the way from Seymour Hall to Marble Arch.

** This article first appeared in London BS-AC's branch magazine following a series of articles in 'Diver' featuring exercise routines including yoga, Canadian army circuit-training, and hypercalisthenics.*

CHAPTER 19: *My initiation as a Dive Marshal*

High Noon at Kimmeridge

The following question will, I am reliably informed, appear in the forthcoming BS-AC National Instructor's Examination . . .

THE PROBLEM:

Bill helped to carry the engines – so he's asking for a place on Boat I. But Colin drove the van down and had to sleep in the lay-by near Taunton. They *could* dive together, but Bill thinks there's something rather creepy about Colin.

This is Alex's second boat dive. She feels confident with Bill. But she thinks there's something rather creepy about Colin. But Colin is a Dive Leader while Bill is only a Sport Diver.

Mervyn is First Class. He's quite happy to take Alex down, but first he has to get air. The dive shop is 20 miles away. They *could* go on Boat II, but Alex is horse-riding at 11.30 with Bill. In any case, Mervyn is down to drive Boat II.

Bill's wife Martine would be positively delighted to dive with Mervyn. This does not escape Bill's notice. Mervyn is less happy about diving with Martine, but he won't say why.

Colin seems particularly eager to dive with Mervyn – but Mervyn thinks there's something rather creepy about Colin. Because he's First Class, however, he fakes a slipped disc. (Bad backs are common among First Class divers).

Unfortunately, Mervyn is one of the two qualified boat-handlers on site. The other is *YOU* – and you're the Marshal. Your assistant could take over, allowing you to drive the boat; but he went off to get petrol over an hour ago with Bill's wife Martine, and, mysteriously, he hasn't returned.

Meanwhile, the branch is breaking up into little knots of muttering malcontents. The lads want their two dives a day. By eleven o'clock, the atmosphere is reminiscent of the day before the Indian Mutiny.

DO YOU:

a. Arrest the trouble-makers and confine them in the van until opening time?
b. Walk naked into the waves in an act of ritual self-extinction?
c. Go horse-riding with Alex?
d. Go horse-riding with Colin?

Compared to your average BS-AC Dive Marshal, Wyatt Earp was a spineless yellow-belly. The Marshal must display the moral courage of Thomas à Beckett and the unerring judgement of Solomon. He must combine Kissinger's tact and diplomacy with Joan Rivers' sense of humour.

When I was finally compelled to marshal a dive as part of my Second Class ticket, I resolved to do the job more thoroughly and imaginatively than it had ever been done before.

I circulated a six-page brochure in advance of the dive. It carried a detailed chart of the waters around Kimmeridge. It analysed the B&B's within a 10-mile radius, allotting stars for breakfasts beyond the call of duty and imposing crippling penalties for nylon sheets.

I'm not a Real Ale buff. I prefer something more substantial – the kind of drink that doesn't spill when you knock it over. Nevertheless, I even included a rundown of the more ethically orientated inns of the locality.

True to my conservationist principles, I explained in bold caps that the area was designated a marine reserve and that on no account must any of the flora or fauna, dead or alive, be removed from its environment.

What did I get for my trouble? At 11am on Day One, Dave (Rambo's less intellectual brother) came charging up the beach with a brace of 3lb lobsters hollering, "The Milky Bars are on me!".

Next morning, the news oozed in like black treacle. Derek was in Swanage General with suspected black water fever. He'd taken my advice and tried a half of Old Ratcatcher in *The Truss and Sneer.* His condition was stable.

Worse, Lee and Sonja, the branch lovers, had sustained second-degree burns – the victims of static electricity generated by the purple brushed nylon sheets at Mrs Bollom's in Ware (a B&B to which I had awarded maximum points for its homemade black pudding and embroidered cotton bed linen). Either Mrs Bollom had been less than frank with me, or she had consciously and unexpectedly decided to move down-market since 1985, perhaps with an eye to the growing C2D socio-economic group.

Otherwise, the dive was reasonably successful. Just the one boat had to be towed back from Poole by a scallop dredger. The skipper, a Mister Drain from Sandbanks, is claiming salvage. The case is due to go to the High Court early next month.

Of course, there was the regrettable incident of the dachshund and the boat pump, but that blew over relatively quickly.

As for the complaints about Letitia's changing arrangements by the Bournemouth Women's Institute coach party, I can only report, without comment, her reply: "People pay good money every Sunday lunchtime at *The Cat and Hacksaw* to see what they've seen. They're lucky I didn't pass the hat round."

The Dorset County Drug Squad were understandably peeved when they raided the dive site. But then they shouldn't have been bugging our VHF traffic. Apparently, it was the reference to "picking up Charlie from the Black Prince" that really set the cat among the pigeons. They released Norman after only twenty-four hours – in fact, as soon as they'd analysed the dusting powder for his drysuit seals.

And quite honestly, I'd told Glenys a thousand times about sticking her spectacle lenses to the outside of her mask with UHU. So I wasn't surprised when she tried to add the 8in artillery shell to her fossil collection. It's just a pity she had to pick a Bank Holiday Monday when the Bomb Disposal Squad felt obliged to clear the beach and the village for more than six hours. The local shopkeepers were understandably concerned, this being the busiest weekend of the season. Fortunately for Glenys, the County Constabulary agreed to smuggle her out to Swanage on the floor of an unmarked car.

No, as I say, my debut as Dive Marshal was relatively uneventful, thank Providence. I don't know how I'd have coped if the kelp had *really* hit the fan.

Happily, I'm now an Advanced Dive Leader (or something), and since I'm deemed to know what I'm doing, it's highly unlikely I'll ever be asked to marshal a dive again.

The Vanishing Goldfish Syndrome

It was my friend Tim Philips who stumbled on the Vanishing Goldfish Syndrome.

Returning to his rooms one evening, he was astonished to discover an empty goldfish bowl. He wasn't astonished to find the bowl, you understand: the bowl was an old friend. It was an established part of his estate. It was the emptiness that was the cause of the astonishment.

Actually, "emptiness" is not strictly accurate. The bowl contained water and weed and a little pink archway where, under happier circumstances, a goldfish might have sported. But that's the point: for "emptiness", read "profound absence of goldfish".

It was a mystery to compare with any of Agatha Christie's. Locked room. Windows closed. No cat. No tell-tale droplets of water on polished mahogany sideboard to imply egress of goldfish – either of its own free will, or through the violent intervention of another party.

After a sleepless night spent in contemplation of the disappearance, Tim Philips toyed with his breakfast. Listlessly, he glanced at the letters page of *The Times.*

"Sir," he read, "Regarding the vanishing of my goldfish in decidedly mystifying circumstances . . .". And the writer went on to describe the fashion of his pet's disappearance, which was almost identical to that of Philips' own experience.

During the following weeks, "The Thunderer" became the forum for hundreds of ex-goldfish owners, each with a bizarre and inexplicable disappearance to report, but none with so much as the germ of a credible explanation. Nor, to my knowledge, has any been offered to this date.

It isn't so much the disappearance of the goldfish that so disturbs me about this rather unsatisfactory story. What's a goldfish here or there, after all? No – it is the profounder implications that are so frightening. What sort of universe is it where goldfish can simply *un-be* at the drop of a hat?

Once you accept the principle as it applies to goldfish, where do you stop? At cats? Or kangaroos? Traffic wardens? Or an inanimate objects – like snorkels?

Which brings me to the real point of these reflections: namely, that somewhere in a parallel universe, among the goldfish, is a mountain of weightbelts, masks, snorkels, knives, watches, car keys – all the valuable items that have inexplicably vanished from the world's dive sites since the invention of the aqualung.

It wasn't that big bloke from Middlesbrough who half-inched your self-honing radar-reflecting net cutters. And if you thought you must have dropped your compass in the gents of *The Laughing Accountant* at Seahouses, think again. They simply slipped through the crack between the dimensions. They were caught in a vortex in the space-time continuum. They were whisked away through a rip in the fabric of reality. They are On The Other Side.

I once "lost" my snorkel at Porthkerris (ie, by a fantastic coincidence, for one infinitessimal fraction of a second, its atomic structure precisely complemented that of the bottom of my dive bag, allowing it to trickle into oblivion like sand through an egg-timer).

Half an hour later I "found" an identical one in thirty metres off the Manacles. Of course, it was not an identical snorkel – it was one and the same snorkel. By an even more fantastic coincidence, it had again osmosed through the cosmic fly-screen which separates the dimensions and returned to our own universe.

That it re-materialised half a mile from the point at which it vanished, I am prepared to overlook. Similarly, I wouldn't mark Shakespeare down for the odd spelling mistake.

Usually, I'm not so lucky. Of the seventy-eight snorkels that have spontaneously "ceased to be" during my diving career, all but one failed to make the return trip.

I was grumbling about the appalling cost of snorkel-loss to a friend from Oxford University BS-AC.

"A senseless waste," he agreed. "But what you need is one of these." And he produced from the inside pocket of his straight-jacket what seemed to be a perfectly ordinary snorkel.

"What's so special about that?" I inquired.

"Drop it among the rocks on a beach: a photo-electric cell in the mouthpiece registers a sudden diminution in light, and a powerful halogen lamp in the barrel emits an unmistakeable flashing orange light. You can see it for miles."

"Cunning." I was impressed. "But what if you drop it on a *sandy* beach? If it was covered in sand, you wouldn't see the light."

"Ah, well. If the photo-electric cell registers a *total* absence of light, it infers that the snorkel might be under sand. As you say, it's a fairly common scenario. It confirms the inference by insinuating a probe – thus – which conducts a micro-chemical analysis of the surrounding medium. If this turns out to consist mainly of silicon, it decides that it's buried in sand and produces a high-pitched warbling sound. You can hear it for miles."

Now I was very impressed. "Very impressive," I conceded. "But suppose you lose it under water. Then what?"

A triumphant smile. Smug, even. "Easy. A device not unlike the human inner ear analyses the motion of the snorkel. If this conforms to certain pre-programmed models, the computer assumes it is submersed in an aquatic medium. But just to be on the safe side, the probe confirms the inference with a micro-chemical sampling procedure. If this registers two parts of hydrogen to one of oxygen, Bob's your Uncle! A capacitor, charged by the photo-electric cell, releases its charge through a tiny motor and a propeller drives the snorkel out of the water back into the boat."

I was sold. "Fantastic. Brilliant!" I said. "I've got to have one! Where did you get it?"

"I found it," he said.

CHAPTER 21: *What do you bother goin' in for?'*

The Old Man and the BC

The Old Man sat on a crumbling capstan watching the divers as they secured their inflatable to the pier and unloaded their equipment.

One of their party, a girl, lingered at the boat searching for her crab hook.

"See anything interestin' down there, did ye?" The Old Man's voice contained a trace of amused irony.

"Not a lot", conceded the girl, "Swanage Harbour is hardly noted for its glorious coral cliffs."

"Then what do ye bother goin' in for?"

She eased her bottle to the ground and smiled. "This is our test weekend. The water's shallow and calm. It suits us very well. But there's nothing much worth seeing."

The Old Man snorted. "Sit down for five minutes an' I'll put that notion out of yer pretty young head for keeps."

A little embarrassed, the Diver obeyed, and the Old Man commenced his tale:

"It was near on fifty years past when Jethro came home from Chinee. He was a sailor, understand, and best pal to me since we were lads.

Well, we had a jug or two down at the *Queen of Bohemia,* and he leans over to me, and he speaks real low. 'What'd ye think if I told ye I'd learned the secret of the fishes?'

"And it turns out he'd met this feller in Chinee who had the knack of breathing underwater. It was a contraption, see, like a pair of wings.

"You strapped 'em on and stuck this tube in yer mouth. And the wings somehow boiled up the sea and turned it into air, clear and sweet as you like.

"Well, I told him he should lay off the ale a bit. But he says no, it's true, on his life. And what's more, he's got the blasted plans to prove it!

"Well, he pulls out a drawing covered all in weird foreign-looking writing and he says, 'You and me, Abe, we're going to make us a couple of these strange-lookin' monstrosities, and we're going to swim about the harbour there like a pair o' porpusses. Won't that be fine?'

"Well, I weren't so sure, but next day we set to work.

"After a month or so, our water wings were near ready. 'Tomorrow, Abe lad', says Jethro, 'we'll go pay our respects to King Neptune!'

"We set out at daybreak in Jethro's cobble and we anchored slap in the middle of the bay – there, straight out 'alf mile or so.

"Jethro went in first, just as the sun came up. He looked proper weird in his water wings – half butterfly, half angel, like Icarus fallin' out of heaven.

"I was proper terrified, I can tell ye. But I spoke a preer, held me breath, and dove in with a mighty crashin' and splashin'. Course, me wings being made all o' brass and iron, I must have weighed near on a half-ton, and I sank like a stone.

"Likely I must've had the gumption to wave me wings about a bit, because before I knew it, I was pulling in air, fresh and sweet as a draught o' Casterbridge cider.

"Anyway, I'm sitting there on the bottom, midst all the crabs and octerpussers. Well, I felt a bit queer for a moment, I can tell ye. It ain't natural, I was thinking, cavorting around without the benefit of God's good air, laughing in the face of Satan himself.

"And then I made out this shape, see, looming towards me, and I thought, here's Jethro, the old dog."

The Old Man puffed at his pipe, lost in recollection

"And was it?" prompted the Diver.

"No", he replied, sadly. "It weren't. It were a mermaid, hang me if it weren't. And a prettier little thing I've yet to meet (yourself apart, of course). All golden, shining tresses and, if you'll pardon me, as trim a little figure as ever broke a man's heart.

"'Come here, Abe Ridout', sez she, 'and follow me!'

"I needed no second prompting. I clinged on that little

green tail of hers like a ferret to a jack rabbit. We fair sped along past whole schools of porpusses and storms of mackerel that would near as swamp yer boat if ye was to charm 'em into yer net.

"Soon we took a turn for the deeps and plummeted down through creatures weird and marvellous to behold. Great eels, there was, with burning lamps for eyes, and whales the sizes of houses, singing sweet as a minster choir.

"Down an' down we went, till all of a sudden we slows up. 'Alright, are ye, lad?' chirps me little mermaid. 'I won't keep ye long. But you were itchin' to play touch-tag with the fishies, and we'd hate for ye to go to all this bother for nothing!'

"Then she curtsies and bids me, 'Welcome to Atlantee!'

"And the weeds moved apart like the drapes in a theatre, and I was so surprised I near forgot to flap me wings! Out there, sitting on the bottom, bold as you like, is the most marvellous place I ever saw. Great towers, there was, soaring up into the blue like blooming cathedrees, an' all the windows sparkling with a dancing sort o' light.

"Me, I felt like a sinner at the gates o' Paradise – I did, truly. I was like to fall flat on me poor face and beg the Lord for His great mercy.

"But me little mermaid bids me arise and says, kindly like, 'Don't worry yeself, Abe, it's only the lost city of Atlantee. You're a lucky feller, you are. There's a few enough folks know Atlantee's down here in Swanage harbour. Them brainy 'uns, professers and the like, they be forever fiddling and fretting about in all sorts of queer Greek places, looking for her. And here she is, in dear ol' Swanage! Marvellous, ain't it?'

"I couldn't help it but agree. What with the glowing of the eels, and the beautiful singing of the whale choirs, it was.

"Then, half-way up the highest tower of all, I saw my pal Jethro hanging out of a window. 'Hello, Abe, old chap', he sez, 'Glad to see ye!'

"But then I spied he weren't wearing his wings no more, and that got me worried.

"Mermaid, sez I, old Jethro there has lost his wings! He'll be hard put to breathe without 'em.

"But, says she, 'Don't fret, Abe. Jethro's as happy as a mouse in a granary. He don't need no wings down here'.

"Well, I sez, it's pushing ten o'clock. It's time we was heading home.

"And she puts an arm round me shoulder and sez 'You'll be going up alone, Abe. Young Jethro's found his true home, now, and he wouldn't thank ye for dragging him away.'"

The Old Man gazed out over the horizon and all that lay beyond it.

Spellbound, the Diver said: "How did you get home?"

"Ah", replied the Old Man. "I don't rightly recall. Next I knows, I'm back in the *Queen of Bohemia,* supping on a jug o' cider.

"A captain's there too, just home from Chinee.

"'You're a friend of young Jethro, aren't ye?' sez he.

"Aye, I reply.

"'Well', sez the captain, 'He charged me to tell ye that he be so taken with Chinee, he's half a mind to settle there. And he sends you his fond regards.'"

The Old Man seemed disinclined to say more. So the Diver rose and slowly followed her comrades along the pier towards the *Queen of Bohemia.*